Hope in the Hard Places

God's Promises and Gifts to the Suffering

Jim & Cindy Powers

ISBN (eBook): 978-1-967120-20-8

ISBN (Paperback): 978-1-967120-19-2

Library of Congress Control Number: 2025918331

Cover art created in CoPilot by Jim Powers.

Cover design by Steve Oros.

Published by Indie Christian Book in Bloomington, Illinois, U.S.A.

www.indiechristianbook.com

CONTENTS

Introduction

You don't have to be suffering to get something out of this book. In fact, we truly hope that you are living your best, most joyous, and most peaceful life. But let's be honest—everyone suffers at some point. Pain and hardship are inevitable in this fallen world. Maybe you picked up this book because you're walking through suffering right now. Maybe you're looking for answers, for hope, for something to hold onto. Or maybe you're simply curious about our story. Whatever brought you here, we're grateful to walk this journey with you.

We, Jim and Cindy, wrote this book because suffering has shaped our lives in ways we never could have imagined. We didn't set out to write a book about trials and hardships—we set out to survive them. But as we look back, we see how God's hand has been with us through it all. And now, we believe our story isn't just ours—it's meant to be shared, to encourage you, and to remind you that no matter what you're facing, you are not alone.

Why We Wrote This Book

We have asked the same question that so many people ask when they are hurting: Why does God allow suffering? If He loves us, why does He permit pain, heartbreak, and loss?

One thing we've learned is that God allows things to happen that create a story He can use. Consider Job. Satan was determined to break him, to make him curse God and turn away. But even in his suffering, Job held on to faith. Now, let's be clear—we aren't comparing our trials to Job's. But we do see a parallel. Like Job, we have endured suffering we never expected. And like Job, we have found that even in the darkest moments, God was still working.

This became undeniable for us on May 10, 2022. Our daughter Miriam was in surgery, and while we waited, we stepped down to the hospital cafeteria for a quick bite. There, we ran into an old friend who was also facing a crisis—one of their adopted children had suffered an injury and was undergoing tests. As we caught up, our friend broke down in tears, sharing the deep struggles they were facing with their children.

Because we had walked through our own struggles with adoption and foster care, we were able to offer more than just words of comfort— we spoke from experience. And that made all the difference. Our friend told us later that hearing from someone who had been there helped her in ways that well-meaning but unrelatable encouragement never could.

That conversation confirmed something for us: Our story needed to be told. Not because we have all the answers, but because when you're in the middle of suffering, you need to know that you're not alone—and that there is hope on the other side.

DOUBT, DARKNESS, AND THE TURNING POINT

Jim

To be honest, we didn't always see things this way. When we were in the middle of our hardest seasons, it didn't feel like God was writing a beautiful story. Many times, I doubted. I wondered if God was even real. I questioned whether He cared, whether He heard my prayers, or whether my suffering had any purpose at all.

There were times when things got better, but there were also times when things got much worse. The lowest season of my life came between 2005 and 2006, and it was then that I came the closest to giving up entirely.

But then, one Sunday, everything changed. Our pastor preached a sermon that shifted my entire perspective. He reminded us that our suffering is not the end of our story. He pointed to the countless examples in Scripture where God took broken people, shattered by suffering, and turned their pain into something beautiful. He urged us to write down our stories—because someone, somewhere, needed to hear that there is life, hope, and joy on the other side of suffering.

Those words stayed with me. And now, years later, this book is our way of passing that message on to you.

What You'll Find in This Book

As we look back over thirty-two years together, we see the fingerprints of God all over our lives. Writing this book has reminded us of the times He stepped in with unmistakable miracles. But we've also recognized the ways He worked quietly, behind the scenes, in ways we only understood later.

Our hope is that by sharing our story, you will be strengthened in your own trials. We pray that your struggles will not be as great as ours have been, but if they are, we want you to know that God will see you through. His Word is full of promises, and if you take the time to study it, you will begin to see His hand at work in your own life.

This book is divided into two parts:

1. **God's Promises to the Suffering** — This section will help you hold on when His promises are all you have. These chapters will encourage you in the times when you are walking by faith and not by sight.
2. **God's Gifts to the Suffering** — This section will show you that suffering is not just about endurance—it's also about transformation. God doesn't just ask us to hold on; He gives us gifts in the middle of the storm. The Holy Spirit

is our Comforter, and He will meet us with strength, peace, and unexpected joy.

A FINAL WORD BEFORE WE BEGIN

We are sharing our story not because we enjoy revisiting the pain, but because we know there is power in testimony. We pray that as you read, you will see that no matter what you are facing, God is faithful. He can provide the strength, courage, and peace you need. And if it is His will, He can and will deliver you from every evil.

We invite you to walk with us through this book—not just as a reader, but as someone whose story is still being written. May this book encourage you, strengthen you, and remind you that no matter how dark things may seem, God is not finished with you yet.

Part One

God's Promises to the Suffering

CHAPTER 1

HE PROMISES OUR SUFFERING

Jim

Have you ever wondered why suffering seems inevitable? When Adam rebelled against God, he didn't just change his own life—he transformed our entire world. He opened the door to a kind of hell on earth that we all experience. Yes, we taste the good life sometimes, those brief glimpses of heaven. But we also walk through valleys so deep and dark they feel like hell itself. And if you're reading this book, chances are you're familiar with those valleys.

Usually, mercifully, the valleys are short-lived, but for some there seems to be a calling to suffer. Certainly, the apostle Paul had that as part of his life: "I will show him how much he must suffer for the sake of my name" (Acts 9:16). No doubt this led to his great statement, "to live is Christ," but "to die is gain" (Philippians 1:21)! And who could forget Job, who said, "Though he slay me, I will hope in him" (Job 13:15).

That we have times of blessing and suffering shouldn't be terribly surprising. Once, God destroyed the earth by a flood because of the depth of corruption and decay He saw upon it. The wages of sin is death, and death is always working. When we experience heaven on earth, it is a blessing. I have experienced such blessings, but without a doubt, my family and I have tasted hell. We have been put through a refiner's fire, and I'll give you the good news straight away: It did not kill us, but strengthened us and prepared us for a glorious heaven someday.

We have been delivered from much of our long suffering. We wait until that ultimate deliverance for ultimate glory, and we hope for more "heaven on earth" as we wait.

As you read our story, you may find yourself asking the one-word question that haunts every sufferer: "Why?" Why did God allow all of this to happen to us, and why did we choose to write this all out for you to read?

IN THIS WORLD, YOU WILL HAVE TROUBLE

Jesus told us in John 16:33,

> I have said these things to you, that in me you may have peace. In the world you will have tribulation. But take heart; I have overcome the world.

While I'm not terribly encouraged to hear that we will have trouble, it gives me great peace to know that in Jesus, we may experience peace because He "has overcome the world." Paul continues the teaching of Jesus in 2 Corinthians 1:9, saying,

> Indeed, we felt that we had received the sentence of death. But that was to make us rely not on ourselves but on God who raises the dead.

Have you ever faced a situation so overwhelming that your own strength simply wasn't enough? That's exactly where God wants us—at the end of ourselves, where we have no choice but to rely on Him completely. You never know; God could be using your suffering to prepare you for what He has planned.

Cindy

I struggle with my health and have for many years. More serious incidents began after I had been married for a few years, with the discovery of a birth defect that doctors wouldn't find out about until I was in my thirties. This was a malformation of my mid-gut. While still in my mother's womb, my intestines were supposed to rotate and settle into their correct places. Mine did not rotate. Instead, they all stayed on one side of my body and began to cause serious complications. I was not able to eat, keep food down, or go to the bathroom regularly, because my intestines were not functioning properly. They had become occluded. However, when I was a child, my parents had never noticed a problem with my eating, and I gained weight normally.

As an adult, I saw several doctors for this problem before one finally did a follow-through study to see how things were being processed through my GI tract. The doctor found the problem instantly and told my husband and me that I had to have this fixed immediately.

Off to surgery I went. I would require nineteen surgeries to get to the point of healing. After the first surgery, I ended up with a staph infection from being in the hospital, which set off a chain reaction of problems and a bunch of additional surgeries to fix the damage. The pain was horrific, so doctors put me on opiate pain control early on, as the pain would prove to be impossible to control without them.

What we didn't know—what nobody warned us about—was that these opiates would slowly reshape my brain, my personality, and our future. The doctors either didn't realize or didn't care about the addictive nature of these medications. They saw my immediate pain and sought to ease it, never imagining they were setting me on a path to a different kind of suffering. Have you ever found that the solution to one problem became the source of something worse? That's exactly what happened to us.

I'd stay on this medication for over ten years and become so addicted that I would go into extreme withdrawals after a few short minutes of not having the regular dose. I slept for hours on end because the medicine made me so tired, and I entered into a deep depression that I wouldn't realize I had until much later. Years went by, and my mind grew darker. I don't remember much about these years, other than a constant battle waging in my mind and deep within my soul.

WHERE THE MEDICAL PROBLEMS BEGAN

While the most serious incidents began with my gut malformation, my first experience with hospitals began in college. I started college in Nebraska, majoring in music education with an emphasis on flute performance. But my health started to decline while I was there. I broke my jaw playing softball, so I had my mouth wired shut during my freshman year of college. My jaw did not heal right, because it was set wrong, and doctors would have to break it again and rewire it shut. At the time, I'm sure I thought it was the worst thing that would happen to me medically. But it wasn't, not by a long shot.

It was years later that we discovered the malformation, or more accurately, the malrotation. Jim tells it this way:

Jim

We were driving home from Colorado, where we had been visiting my parents for Christmas. This was always the highlight of our year. Whenever we couldn't go, it was painful. To be able to play in the snow and see Grandma and Grandpa was such a treat for all of us. Since I worked for a school district, I was fortunate to have two weeks off around Christmas, so we always stayed with Grandma and Grandpa the entire holiday. When it was time to return home, we loaded the van and drove back to Texas, a long fourteen-to-sixteen hour drive; the kids' frequent potty stops made it such a long day. This time, about an hour away from home, our lives would be turned upside down by horrific effects that would last for years to come.

During the drive, Cindy doubled over with extreme abdominal pain. I got everyone home and unloaded the van while Cindy waited in the van in agony. Since our daughter Mary was old enough at this point to babysit, I took Cindy to the emergency room. The hospital ran their usual tests and, based on her symptoms, discovered that Cindy's gallbladder was diseased and had to be removed. They did emergency surgery to remove the gallbladder and sent her home.

This should have been an easy, routine surgery and recovery. But a week later, Cindy was still in agonizing pain. She went back to see the surgeon, and he gave her more pain medicine and told her to come back in two weeks. It was two weeks of torture as the pain increased even more. I accompanied her to the doctor, and he suggested there was one more test to do but was certain it would not show anything.

Cindy was scheduled for this procedure, a live x-ray during which she drank barium as a contrast. The test was intended to show whether or not the barium would pass all the way through her digestive tract. Cindy recalls that during the test, the technician and radiologist were pointing and speaking very quietly. After the test was done, she was sent home.

Not more than a couple of hours later, the surgeon called Cindy and said she had to come back in right away, so I left work to go with her. This was when they told us they had found Cindy's intestinal malrotation. Essentially, everything between her stomach and large bowel was twisted so food could not pass, which was causing the extreme pain. The surgeon said if she didn't have surgery to correct the condition, she would die. The surgery was scheduled for 7:00 a.m. the next morning. From the waiting room, I watched family after family of other patients come and go while I waited. Around 4:00 p.m., the surgeon finally came out and told me the procedure went well. Thankfully, none of her intestines had developed gangrene, so he didn't have to remove any, which, he noted, was unusual.

Intestinal malrotation has a mortality rate of greater than 90% in infants within their first week of life. They can't get the nutrition they need to survive and thrive. Some infants survive after surgery, and a few more survive into adulthood, as Cindy had done. As we continued to read about this condition, we found it is caused during development in the uterus. In the first trimester of development, the baby doesn't have room in the abdominal cavity for the intestines, so they develop outside while the body grows. Around the end of the first trimester, the body draws the intestines in, and in most cases, they rotate so everything is properly lined up. In cases of intestinal malrotation, the intestines don't rotate, leaving them twisted to varying degrees. There is an assumption that some adults live to old age with the condition, never knowing they had any problems.

Cindy stayed in the hospital for a couple of days after the surgery to make sure her digestive system would recover and was sent home on pain medications. If only we'd known then what we would so painfully discover years later about those opiates. The next week, I took her for her follow up.

ABUSE FROM THE DOCTOR

Cindy's surgeon was not in the office, so a fellow surgeon examined her and found she had an infection in the surgical site. I still can't believe what happened next. Instead of giving anything to deaden the pain, the doctor simply tore Cindy's belly back open right there in the office. She took samples, and the lab confirmed Cindy had MRSA in the wound, so she was scheduled for another surgery to debride the infection. MRSA is a nasty staph infection that has become resistant to most antibiotics. Patients of invasive surgeries can develop MRSA when medical staff don't wash thoroughly enough before touching the patient.

This surgery was the first of eighteen more that would span the next five years and cause unspeakable pain for Cindy. Each surgery brought not just physical agony but emotional trauma as well. Can you imagine going through procedure after procedure, hoping each time that it would be the last, only to face another complication? Doctors either had to debride the infection or attempt to repair the abdominal hernia that had developed.

In December 2004, she had one of the surgeries to debride the infection after the last hernia repair. Surgeons also attempted to put another piece of mesh in her belly to repair the hernia. Within just a couple of weeks, she had already badly re-infected, so they once again debrided the infection and removed the mesh. This time, they left the wound open and put a wound vac in place to slowly suck out the infection. Along with high doses of very powerful antibiotics, they hoped this would give her a clean belly to repair again in the future. Since I am describing this somewhat clinically, you may be tempted to underestimate how horrible this all was. Don't. It was terrible, and things got worse.

From Bad to Worse

One time when Cindy was admitted, the doctor had placed a central line in the artery just above her right lung. What nobody knew was that one of the lines had punctured the lung cavity. Since Cindy couldn't eat, they added IV nourishment to her regimen. The nurse connected the milky substance to the third port and started it running. By about 3:00 a.m. the next morning, Cindy was gasping to breathe. She called me at home, so I called the nurse to question their care. The nurse assured me they would take good care of her, so I went back to sleep. At about 6:30 that morning, I received another call from the hospital and was told to get there right away. I dressed for work and left as quickly as I could. At this time, we were homeschooling our oldest child, Mary. Since she didn't have to be at school, I left our other two children, Jacob and Phoebe, with Mary at home.

When I got to the hospital, I went up to the ICU and was met by the pulmonologist who had been called in. He discovered the central line issue and acted quickly to drain the cavity. Because the experience is so painful and frightening, he put Cindy in a drug-induced coma while the cavity drained, and until her breathing returned to normal. She spent two days in the ICU before returning to her regular room. She was now in incredible pain from both her belly and the hole in her right lung cavity.

Doctors struggled to get her pain to a manageable level, adding higher and higher doses of very dangerous narcotics. This would have a long-lasting impact on Cindy and on our family. There is no way we could have known what was coming, but even now, I'm not sure what we could have done differently at the time. She was simply in a living nightmare.

When it became apparent Cindy would not be coming home for Christmas, I called her sister, and we put together plans to take Christmas to her in the hospital. She was upset that she couldn't be at home with our tree and decorations but was especially crushed that we couldn't make our annual trip back to Colorado. My parents understood and sent gifts down to us for the kids.

Christmas morning brought happy sounds to our house. I woke up with the children and discovered what Santa Claus had brought to them. I made sure to capture it on video so that Cindy could experience it later. After some chaos, Mary and I prepared the hot foods that we would be taking to the hospital. We carefully packed up the food and gifts and headed to the hospital. Cindy's sister and family arrived about the same time, so we all descended on the family room and converted it to the best make-shift holiday experience we could create. Cindy was heavily drugged from the pain medication, but the photos and videos showed that she had a good time and enjoyed our company. The kids took it in stride and made the best out of a not-so-perfect situation. We stayed for the better part of the day, at least long enough to eat a second meal before heading home.

Days later, the kids and I went back to the hospital to visit Cindy. She was extremely drowsy from the pain medications. At this point, she had on 175 mcg in Fentanyl patches, a drug that, at the time, was usually only used for cancer patients in their final stages of life to control the pain. The doctors also had IV dilaudid ordered for breakthrough pain. When I asked the nurse about her dosage, she told me if they had put this much opiates on a horse cold turkey, the horse would die. I think her comparison was intended to shock me, which it did.

This won't be the end of the story about Cindy's health problems or the issues caused by the opiate addiction that she developed as a result of the extremely high doses of pain medication. But we'll pause for now to further examine the idea of suffering. The title of this chapter is, "He Promises Our Suffering." This is a very off-putting idea for most. But the way we look at it is that when suffering comes, it shouldn't be surprising. We wrote above about how Jesus promised we would suffer in this world, but that we should take heart, because He has overcome the world. But where else does the Bible indicate that suffering will be part of the human experience? Let's look at a few places in Scripture.

IN THE BEGINNING...

The original design for the world was that there would be no suffering. In the beginning, God created the heavens and earth and everything in them and called all of it "good" and "very good." He created man good and sinless in His image and gave him the work of subduing the earth and ruling over it. He placed the man and his wife in a paradisal garden and called him to tend the lush garden that would so easily give up its fruit.

BUT THEN...EVIL

The evil one however, also found his way into the paradise God created. Before you ask, we don't know precisely why God allowed Satan into His garden, but we do believe He allowed it. Just as we believe He allows our suffering, we believe He allowed this temptation to come to Eve. Why? We don't exactly know. We could guess that free will demands that Adam and Eve have a genuine option to rebel against God, and true love demands a genuine option to leave love unrequited. We know there is some reason God allowed it, or it wouldn't have happened, but we can't say for sure anything that God doesn't say for sure in the Bible, and in this case, He doesn't say. Here's what happened:

> Now the serpent was more crafty than any other beast of the field that the Lord God had made.
>
> He said to the woman, "Did God actually say, 'You shall not eat of any tree in the garden'?" And the woman said to the serpent, "We may eat of the fruit of the trees in the garden, but God said, 'You shall not eat of the fruit of the tree that is in the midst of the garden, neither shall you touch it, lest you die.'" But the serpent said to the woman, "You will not surely die. For God knows that when you eat of it your eyes will be opened, and you will be like God, knowing good and evil." So when the woman saw that the tree was good for food, and that it was a delight to the eyes, and that the tree was to be desired to make one wise, she took of its

fruit and ate, and she also gave some to her husband who was with her, and he ate. Then the eyes of both were opened, and they knew that they were naked. And they sewed fig leaves together and made themselves loincloths.

And they heard the sound of the Lord God walking in the garden in the cool of the day, and the man and his wife hid themselves from the presence of the Lord God among the trees of the garden. But the Lord God called to the man and said to him, "Where are you?" And he said, "I heard the sound of you in the garden, and I was afraid, because I was naked, and I hid myself." He said, "Who told you that you were naked? Have you eaten of the tree of which I commanded you not to eat?" The man said, "The woman whom you gave to be with me, she gave me fruit of the tree, and I ate." Then the Lord God said to the woman, "What is this that you have done?" The woman said, "The serpent deceived me, and I ate."

The Lord God said to the serpent,
      "Because you have done this,
          cursed are you above all livestock
          and above all beasts of the field;
      on your belly you shall go,
          and dust you shall eat
          all the days of your life.
      I will put enmity between you and the woman,
          and between your offspring and her offspring;
      he shall bruise your head,
          and you shall bruise his heel."

To the woman he said,
      "I will surely multiply your pain in childbearing;
          in pain you shall bring forth children.
      Your desire shall be for your husband,

and he shall rule over you."

And to Adam he said,
    "Because you have listened to the voice of your wife
        and have eaten of the tree
    of which I commanded you,
        'You shall not eat of it,'
    cursed is the ground because of you;
        in pain you shall eat of it all the days of your life;
    thorns and thistles it shall bring forth for you;
        and you shall eat the plants of the field.
    By the sweat of your face
        you shall eat bread,
    till you return to the ground,
        for out of it you were taken;
    for you are dust,
        and to dust you shall return."
The man called his wife's name Eve, because she was the mother of all living. And the Lord God made for Adam and for his wife garments of skins and clothed them.

Then the Lord God said, "Behold, the man has become like one of us in knowing good and evil. Now, lest he reach out his hand and take also of the tree of life and eat, and live forever—" therefore the Lord God sent him out from the garden of Eden to work the ground from which he was taken. He drove out the man, and at the east of the garden of Eden he placed the cherubim and a flaming sword that turned every way to guard the way to the tree of life.

— Genesis 3:1-24 ESV

What a tragic mess. Work will be hard, childbirth will bring suffering, marriage will be hard, and no more life in paradise. Adam and Eve would have kids, and parenting them would be hard (one of their sons kills the other). Suffering and pain.

Have you ever noticed how much of the Bible's story hinges on this moment in the Garden? Everything changed when sin entered the world. The harmony between God and humanity was shattered, the relationship between husband and wife was strained, and creation itself was placed under a curse. Suddenly, the world became a place where suffering wasn't an exception—it was the rule.

NOAH

As you read through the Bible, you'll find that it doesn't shy away from suffering. It's brutally honest. After Adam's fall, humanity spiraled downward. Evil spread like a virus until God's heart broke over what His creation had become. Can you imagine the pain God felt seeing the world He lovingly created become so corrupted that He chose to wash it away with a flood? This isn't just unrelatable ancient history; it reveals something profound about suffering: It's woven into the very fabric of our fallen world.

> The Lord saw that the wickedness of man was great in the earth, and that every intention of the thoughts of his heart was only evil continually. And the Lord regretted that he had made man on the earth, and it grieved him to his heart. So the Lord said, "I will blot out man whom I have created from the face of the land, man and animals and creeping things and birds of the heavens, for I am sorry that I have made them."
>
> — GENESIS 6:5-7

There was so much evil in the world that God destroyed everyone and started over. Cindy and I are Christians, and we hold fast to a faith in the goodness and sovereignty of God. I have heard scholars say that the people of Noah's day were no worse than we are today, but I doubt it. With the presence of the "sons of God" on the earth in such a physical way that they could procreate with the "daughters of men" (Genesis 6:1-4), I think the level of demonic activity was beyond anything we could imagine. These passages are mysterious, but they show that tragedy and suffering go with the human experience.

JOB

From the time of Noah, we see much trouble for the people of the world, so much so that one of the blessed and chosen patriarchs says this of his life: "Few and evil have been the days of the years of my life, and they have not attained to the days of the years of the life of my fathers in the days of their sojourning" (Genesis 47:9).

What scholars say is one of the oldest books in the Bible actually comes later in the order. Job is a name synonymous with suffering, and for good reason. Job has a special place in our hearts, because on some level we have experienced many of the same afflictions, though not quite to the same degree. Here's what the Bible says at the beginning of the book of Job:

Now there was a day when the sons of God came to present themselves before the Lord, and Satan also came among them. The Lord said to Satan, "From where have you come?" Satan answered the Lord and said, "From going to and fro on the earth, and from walking up and down on it." And the Lord said to Satan, "Have you considered my servant Job, that there is none like him on the earth, a blameless and upright man, who fears God and turns away from evil?" Then Satan answered the Lord and said, "Does Job fear God for no reason? Have you not put a hedge around him and his house and all that he has, on every side? You have blessed the work of his hands, and his possessions have increased in the land. But stretch out your hand and touch all that he has, and he will curse you to your face." And the Lord said to Satan, "Behold, all that he has is in your hand. Only against him do not stretch out your hand." So Satan went out from the presence of the Lord.

— JOB 1:6-12

Have you ever felt like your life was somehow the subject of a cosmic conversation? Like forces beyond your understanding were at work in your suffering? Job's story reveals something both unsettling and comforting: Satan is the author of calamity, but he cannot act apart from God's permission.

DAVID

For another example of this, consider the story of David when he ordered Joab, his nephew and the commander of his armies, to take a census of the fighting men. For reasons I don't entirely understand, God had forbidden this counting. Perhaps God thought it showed a lack of trust in Himself. Here's the story in 2 Samuel 24:1-15:

> Again the anger of the Lord was kindled against Israel, and he incited David against them, saying, "Go, number Israel and Judah." So the king said to Joab, the commander of the army, who was with him, "Go through all the tribes of Israel, from Dan to Beersheba, and number the people, that I may know the number of the people." But Joab said to the king, "May the Lord your God add to the people a hundred times as many as they are, while the eyes of my lord the king still see it, but why does my lord the king delight in this thing?" But the king's word prevailed against Joab and the commanders of the army. So Joab and the commanders of the army went out from the presence of the king to number the people of Israel. They crossed the Jordan and began from Aroer, and from the city that is in the middle of the valley, toward Gad and on to Jazer. Then they came to Gilead, and to Kadesh in the land of the Hittites; and

they came to Dan, and from Dan they went around to Sidon, and came to the fortress of Tyre and to all the cities of the Hivites and Canaanites; and they went out to the Negeb of Judah at Beersheba. So when they had gone through all the land, they came to Jerusalem at the end of nine months and twenty days. And Joab gave the sum of the numbering of the people to the king: in Israel there were 800,000 valiant men who drew the sword, and the men of Judah were 500,000.

But David's heart struck him after he had numbered the people. And David said to the Lord, "I have sinned greatly in what I have done. But now, O Lord, please take away the iniquity of your servant, for I have done very foolishly." And when David arose in the morning, the word of the Lord came to the prophet Gad, David's seer, saying, "Go and say to David, 'Thus says the Lord, Three things I offer you. Choose one of them, that I may do it to you.'" So Gad came to David and told him, and said to him, "Shall three years of famine come to you in your land? Or will you flee three months before your foes while they pursue you? Or shall there be three days' pestilence in your land? Now consider, and decide what answer I shall return to him who sent me." Then David said to Gad, "I am in great distress. Let us fall into the hand of the Lord, for his mercy is great; but let me not fall into the hand of man."

So the Lord sent a pestilence on Israel from the morning until the appointed time. And there died of the people from Dan to Beersheba 70,000 men.

This is tragic. Though we can't easily understand why God was mad about David's desire to count the fighting men, it is obvious that David understood and knew he'd done wrong. Here is a case of suffering because of one's own sin. But even harder to grasp is that it is a case of 70,000 men dying, and countless others grieving their deaths, because of the sin of their leader. This speaks to the corporate nature of humanity, first seen when Adam fell and the whole world, of which he was the steward, paid the price. When you are suffering, it may be due not to your sin, but to some other sin in history. But take heart, because the whole point of such corporate representation is that by one man's death, all will be made alive!

This story about David is told twice in the Bible. Most of the stories found in 1 and 2 Chronicles can also be found in 1 and 2 Samuel and 1 and 2 Kings. Look at this story of David counting his fighting men in 1 Chronicles 21:1-2. We'll just examine the first part:

> Then Satan stood against Israel and incited David to number Israel. So David said to Joab and the commanders of the army, "Go, number Israel, from Beersheba to Dan, and bring me a report, that I may know their number."

Wait! What? But didn't the writer of 2 Samuel say that it was God who did it? This is what I'm trying to illustrate. God cannot do evil. When 2 Samuel said God incited David, it had simplified the account. God doesn't tempt us, but Satan does (James 1:13). But if you don't think that God would *desire* someone to be tempted, then how do you explain the temptation of Christ in the wilderness?

> And Jesus, full of the Holy Spirit, returned from the Jordan and was led by the Spirit in the wilderness for forty days, being tempted by the devil. And he ate nothing during those days. And when they were ended, he was hungry.

> — LUKE 4:1-2

FINDING PURPOSE IN YOUR SUFFERING

I've found that when suffering hits hardest, the question "Why?" can become a prison. It can paralyze us, keeping us stuck in an endless loop of confusion and anger. What if we shifted our focus? What if, in the midst of your pain, you held tight to these life-giving truths:

1. God is sovereign over the universe, and Satan is not allowed to go beyond whatever limits God places over him.
2. God is love, and He loves you.
3. God is your perfect Father who will use whatever you are going through for your ultimate good.
4. You will have the choice each time you suffer to use it to grow, or to stagnate in victimhood.

We choose growth and refinement. The Bible likens the growth that happens through pain and suffering to gold in the refiner's fire.

> In this you rejoice, though now for a little while, if necessary, you have been grieved by various trials, so that the tested genuineness of your faith—more precious than gold that perishes though it is tested by fire—may be found to result in praise and glory and honor at the revelation of Jesus Christ.
>
> — 1 Peter 1:6-7

Did God allow your suffering? Of course, or it wouldn't be happening. Does that mean He isn't good? No, it doesn't. Some of you may remember this Sunday school tune:

Jesus loves me, this I know, for the Bible tells me so...

What would happen if you accepted completely that you need to go through what you need to go through, and that ultimately, it will turn out for your good? Romans 8:18-25 says:

> For I consider that the sufferings of this present time are not worth comparing with the glory that is to be revealed to us. For the creation waits with eager longing for the revealing of the sons of God. For the creation was subjected to futility,

not willingly, but because of him who subjected it, in hope that the creation itself will be set free from its bondage to corruption and obtain the freedom of the glory of the children of God. For we know that the whole creation has been groaning together in the pains of childbirth until now. And not only the creation, but we ourselves, who have the first-fruits of the Spirit, groan inwardly as we wait eagerly for adoption as sons, the redemption of our bodies. For in this hope we were saved. Now hope that is seen is not hope. For who hopes for what he sees? But if we hope for what we do not see, we wait for it with patience.

Paul, author of this passage, encourages other sufferers that suffering produces "glory to be revealed in us," which far outweighs the suffering of the present. The whole creation suffers, he says, and the whole creation will be transformed when the "children of God" "obtain the freedom and glory" that God has in store for them. It would seem that sometimes freedom and glory come through our afflictions. We "hope for what we do not see," and "we wait for it with patience."

Sometimes, the only solace we have when we suffer is that God has promised that this world is a place of suffering, but that no suffering is wasted. In that, we take heart, even as we cry out for deliverance. We ask for deliverance, but also for patience to endure and for grace to believe in the glory to be revealed in us at the end. Jesus said we would have suffering in this world, but that He has overcome the world. By His grace, so do we.

Chapter 2

He Promises His Presence

Cindy

When I was twelve, my sister married a guy she met at the grocery store where she worked. My parents, realizing they couldn't stop her in spite of her youth, consented. She was only sixteen, and her husband was eighteen. After the wedding, which took place in a park, they moved to a small basement apartment in Ft. Morgan, Colorado, somehow getting by with a twin bed and not much to their names. I would often go to my sister's house after school and during the summer and stay with her for several weeks at a time.

Next to the apartment building was a home belonging to a widower named Chester, a man in his fifties. My sister and I often sat on his front porch with him, drinking lemonade or tea and talking for hours. Chester seemed lonely but friendly. We got to know him quite well over the following months, and he became somewhat of a friend.

One afternoon, my sister and I were at Chester's house talking, and my sister said she needed to go to the grocery store. Chester said I could stay there with him for a bit while she picked up a few things they needed. She left me there and went to the store.

After some time, Chester asked if I wanted to come in and see his wife's things. He hadn't packed up anything of his late wife's, so there were fine china and various other items around the house. As we walked through the rooms, he'd reminisce about one thing or another, being friendly as usual and walking with a cane. I could hear the click of the cane just before I heard the stomp of his foot as it landed on the carpeted floors. The carpet was long, shag-like, and dull yellow and looked as though it had been there for many years.

We progressed through the home, and Chester came upon the door to the basement and opened it. He started down the stairs, first his cane and then a step down, until he reached the bottom step. We looked through each room, taking the time to look at all of the items he cherished in his lifetime. There was one room left, and it was in a corner of the basement toward the back of the house. The bed was nicely made and appeared soft, with a chenille bedspread on it. The bedspread was a medium blue, with those familiar knot-like structures all over.

In an instant, everything changed. Have you ever had a moment when your entire world shifted? When safety suddenly became danger? The kind, gentle man I thought I knew vanished before my eyes, replaced by someone cold and calculating. The transformation was so complete that my young mind couldn't process what was happening.

He tossed his cane aside and shoved me down onto the bed. I remember the feel of the bedspread beneath me, its texture strangely vivid as he restrained me with a belt and a piece of rope he had taken from the closet. My mind struggled to comprehend what was happening, clinging to small, insignificant details as a way to escape the overwhelming fear and confusion.

I was paralyzed. I couldn't move, speak, or understand how everything had changed so quickly. The trust I had felt moments earlier shattered in an instant, replaced by a growing sense of dread.

What happened next was something I couldn't have imagined, let alone understood. Chester violated my trust and my body, disregarding my fear and confusion. He acted with calculated cruelty, using words that blamed me for his actions, compounding my bewilderment. I didn't have the words or knowledge to label what he was doing, but I could feel the deep emotional and physical pain, a pain I thought I wouldn't survive.

When it was over, his anger turned into further violence. He struck me repeatedly with the belt, each blow leaving me more stunned and broken. I couldn't understand why he was doing this. My young mind searched desperately for answers, wondering if I had somehow done something to deserve this cruelty.

Then, as suddenly as it began, it ended. Chester stormed out of the room, slamming the door behind him. I lay there, listening to the sound of his footsteps receding down the basement hall—the tap of his cane and the heavy thud of his stride—until the house fell silent again.

The silence was almost worse than the beating and rape. I felt all alone and could not move at all, and since he'd tied my feet and hands so tightly, I could not free myself. I tried to wiggle this way and pull that way, and cried out loud, because the pain was horrible from him being inside me and also from my hands and ankles being bound so tightly. I cried for a long time. I don't know exactly how much time went by, but the light began to dim to darkness. The small window near the ceiling that once showed a small amount of light was now pitch black, and the room was darker than any place I'd ever been. As I cried, I thought I would be rescued any minute, that my sister would surely come to get me. In my childhood naivety, I was certain that she would know that I was tied up in the basement and rescue me. I thought that maybe this was a joke they were playing on me.

But the darkness persisted, and no one rescued me. I fell asleep for a while and woke up confused as to where I was. Then, I realized that this wasn't a bad dream. It was real. I didn't hear footprints upstairs anymore. I wondered if Chester was asleep. I thought if I screamed now, maybe my sister would hear me, or he would come and let me go. Then I thought that maybe he'd get upset and beat me again with that belt. I felt like sounds would not come out of my mouth, even if I tried. This time, wiggling loosened the ropes a little bit. They were not so tight now, or maybe I had become used to the tightness on my wrists and ankles.

I heard the doorbell ring several times, and that is the moment I found my voice. I screamed as loudly as I could, calling my sister's name. In the darkness, looking around, I saw that small window above the bed. I decided I had to get out of the house before Chester could come back and hurt me again. I finally managed to get my hands free. The bed was near the window, and the headboard to the bed went more than halfway up to the window. I decided to see if I could get it open and get out of there.

I escaped through that window.

In those days, rape was not talked about. When it was talked about, people would tend to blame the girl for dressing too skimpy or leading the man on, and it was shameful to the family and to the victim. I did tell my parents what happened, and all I knew was that my dad took care of the problem himself. I never saw Chester again. We didn't talk about it as a family. To this day, I'm not sure what happened.

Years later, my sister doesn't remember much about the incident. I have had to remind her of the details. She doesn't remember a lot from her years growing up. So many years have passed now, but healing took a long time. The trauma stayed with me for many years after I got married.

After that incident, things went somewhat back to normal for a while, and I lived the life of a normal kid. Childhood brains are funny in how they can compartmentalize. Trauma like that will get filed away like a time bomb. It would have been a game changer if my parents had understood and gotten me help right away, but like most parents of that generation, they had no idea what to do. I don't blame them, but I hope that going forward, parents understand how crucial it is to get help for their children.

TRIGGERED

Once, my husband took his belt off similarly to how Chester did at the time he tied me up and raped me. That triggered a series of memories that I would need counseling to get through, and my sweet husband walked this road with me all the way through. I can talk about the experience without tears or fear of the bad memories now. I believe the point when you know healing has happened is when you can talk about the incident without strong emotions taking over. It should be mentioned, however, that some people shut down so much emotionally after trauma that they can't feel anything about it. This response doesn't mean they're healed, only that the trauma is locked away—for a time.

Where Was God?

Where was God? It's the question that haunts every survivor of trauma, every person who has faced unspeakable pain. It's a question I asked. Jim asked it when he learned what had happened to me. And you've probably asked this question too, in your own moments of darkness. This chapter is about the promise that has sustained me through decades of healing: God was there. He didn't look away. He didn't abandon me. And friend, He hasn't abandoned you either.

Jim

What happened to Cindy was horrific, evil, gross, and should never have happened to anyone, let alone a little girl. But the truth is that horrific things take place every minute of every day somewhere in the world. When it comes home to our own loved ones and our own lives, these questions become the focus of our thoughts. Where is God? What is He doing while people are being raped, beaten, and oppressed? Where was He when people were enslaved and mistreated in every generation since the Fall? Where was He when so-called "natural disasters" wiped out millions in one day? He has been here, right here, all along.

I don't know why God allows evil, but I do know He doesn't look away. I know He has an ultimate plan to eradicate it. I don't know why He is waiting to complete that plan, but I know that if He took away pain right now, everyone you know who doesn't know Him yet would die in their sins and perish in hell.

I know God was there when Cindy was being raped and beaten by that evil man, when she was in crippling pain from countless medical issues, and when she was severely addicted to pain meds and in an absolute pit of despair. I know He was there in a world where the only way for us to be image bearers, human, is to have the free will to sin against Him and others. For God to intervene in the way we would like Him to would be the end of reason and agency. It would be the end of free will. It would be the end of love. Real love.

God must heal the world in a way that keeps those elements intact, and this way had something to do with the betrayal, torture, and death of His own Son on the cross. God's plan has a timeline, but until it is accomplished, God is there in the deepest, darkest, and most secret places of sin and evil, watching, keeping score for the judgment, and being present with the suffering, knowing Himself what it is to suffer.

INVISIBLE

I'll be honest with you—one of the most challenging aspects of trusting God through suffering is that we can't see Him with our physical eyes. When pain overwhelms us, we long for a visible Savior, someone we can touch, whose presence is undeniable. But faith asks us to trust what we cannot see. The author of Hebrews reminds us that "faith is the assurance of things hoped for, the conviction of things not seen" (Hebrews 11:1). What does this mean for you and me in our darkest moments?

This means that we have to grapple with the invisibility of God. God has always been there in your suffering, but you couldn't see Him. One passage that comes to mind that illustrates this truth is in the beautiful but complicated book of Hosea. Hosea was an Old Testament prophet, which means he was one of the very small (minuscule, even) number of humans who heard the audible voice of God.

As an aside, most people who heard or saw God physically were called to incredibly difficult things. It's one thing to suffer for God, but it's another thing to be sent into suffering. Cindy and I have realized in hindsight our "call to suffer," but I'm glad God didn't pull us aside early and say, "You two are going to suffer now," which is exactly what He does for many people in the Bible, such as Paul: "I will show him how much he must suffer for my name" (Acts 9:16 NIV), as well as Hosea. Hosea was told by God he was going to have a bad marriage. In fact, God said,

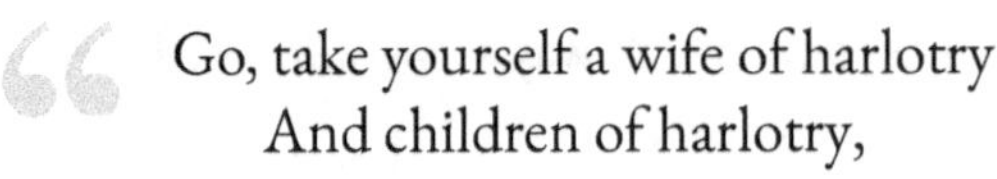

> Go, take yourself a wife of harlotry
>   And children of harlotry,

For the land has committed great harlotry
By departing from the Lord.

— HOSEA 1:2 NKJV

God wanted Hosea to show the Israelites that He considers them to be an adulterous wife. This is why he calls Hosea to have an adulterous wife. Imagine your wedding to someone God already told you was going to cheat on you and run away with another man.

But God says something else in this about the way He cares for people and continues to provide for them even when they turn away from Him.

Therefore, behold,
I will hedge up your way with thorns,
And wall her in,
So that she cannot find her paths.
She will chase her lovers,
But not overtake them;
Yes, she will seek them, but not find them.
Then she will say,
'I will go and return to my first husband,
For then it was better for me than now.'
For she did not know
That I gave her grain, new wine, and oil,
And multiplied her silver and gold—
Which they prepared for Baal.

— HOSEA 2:6-8 NKJV

Do you see what God is saying? He describes His plan to bring Israel back to Himself by frustrating her plans. Verse 8 says, "she did not know that I gave her grain, new wine, and oil, and multiplied her silver and gold—which they prepared for Baal." God says that the Israelites were worshiping Baal with the very provisions given to them by God.

How does this relate to suffering? First, it promises that we suffer for all sorts of reasons. Hosea's wife, Gomer, suffered because she was committing adultery. Hosea suffered because God had called him to suffer so he could deliver the message to Israel through the object lesson of his life. The thing we learn relevant to this present discussion on the presence of God in our suffering is that God is always there. He is not only there, but He still intervenes and provides. The very next passage tells us how He stopped providing in order to bring Gomer, and ultimately the Israelites, home to Himself. This reminds us of the prodigal son whose suffering led him to "come to himself" and go home to his father to seek mercy (Luke 15:17-20).

OUR JOB TO POINT OUT THE PRESENCE OF THE LORD

As Cindy and I look back at our story—the abuse, the addiction, the medical trauma, the losses—we can now see what was once hidden from us: God was there every step of the way. Every. Single. Step. And friend, He is with you too, right now, in whatever darkness you're facing. If we can help you recognize His presence in your own story, if we can shine a light on the ways He's already working in your life, then this book will have fulfilled its purpose, because you're not alone. You never have been.

In his book *Finding God in Unexpected Places*, author Philip Yancey introduces the topic of God's presence in suffering with a story of a woman named Joanna in South Africa. He says,

In Cape Town, I met Joanna Flanders-Thomas, a dynamic woman of mixed race. As a student she had agitated against the apartheid government. After that nationwide victory she turned to a local problem, the most violent prison in South Africa, where Nelson Mandela had spent eight years of confinement.

Joanna started visiting prisoners daily, bringing them a simple gospel message of forgiveness and reconciliation. She earned their trust, got them to talk about their abusive childhoods, and showed them a better way of resolving conflicts. The year before her visits began, the prison recorded 279 acts of violence against inmates and guards; the next year there were two.

Joanna's results attracted the attention of BBC producers, who sent a camera crew from London to film two one-hour documentaries on her work.

I met Joanna and her husband at a restaurant on the waterfront of Cape Town. "I've seen the BBC documentaries, but I still don't get it," I said. "These guys are monsters—rapists, murderers. And from what I could see you were simply holding Bible studies, playing trust games, having prayer meetings. What really happened to transform Pollsmoor Prison?" Joanna looked up and said, almost without thinking, 'Well, of course, Philip, God was already present in the prison. I just had to make him visible."

Joanna's offhand comment became for me a mission statement of how to live as an adult follower of Jesus.[*]

We feel the same. God was in our lives and our situation every step of the way, and He is in yours too. If we can point Him out to you, we will have fulfilled at least one important part of our purpose on this earth. In fact, we believe that God counts on us to point out His presence.

In the book of Genesis, we are told about the creation of mankind: "Then God said, 'Let us make man in our image, after our likeness'" (Genesis 1:26a). Some people believe that God forbids His people to make images of Him for any reason, especially to worship. But many don't realize that God has already crafted an image of Himself. He made man in His image. That is incredible for more reasons than we can come up with, but one that we can come up with is that He wanted all of creation to be able to look at a man or woman and get an idea of what God is like. He wants us to be able to point out His presence, His likeness, the truth of His existence in one another. Not only that, but He

---

[*] Philip Yancey, *Finding God in Unexpected Places.* Doubleday Religious Publishing Group, 2005.

wants us to be able to point out His presence in the things He created. Paul said that humans have no excuse to disbelieve God, because God is everywhere, and the evidence of Him is everywhere for us to point out. Romans 1:19-21 says,

 For what can be known about God is plain to them, because God has shown it to them. For his invisible attributes, namely, his eternal power and divine nature, have been clearly perceived, ever since the creation of the world, in the things that have been made. So they are without excuse. For although they knew God, they did not honor him as God or give thanks to him, but they became futile in their thinking, and their foolish hearts were darkened.

Part of our job is to point out His presence by living out our destiny as His image bearers and acting like Him. This is being a disciple of Jesus. We are pointing to His "invisible attributes" that are "clearly perceived...in the things that have been made." We can make a powerful difference in the world by pointing to the presence of God.

In the South African prison when the murder rate was high, Joanna came and did what she was called to do: point out God's presence. God was also present in that dark and terrible basement of Cindy's hell with Chester. I can only imagine His grief that His creation would do such a thing to one another. God has been forced to look upon all the evil that humans have done to one another since Adam gave us over to Satan.

Think about this: Any one of us is traumatized by witnessing just one act of evil. We even imagine you might need some time today to get over reading Cindy's horrific story. But God was not only in that room with Cindy and Chester; He was also in every dark place on the globe, witnessing every tragic situation all at once. Only the infinite God of the universe could absorb such pain and suffering. We always want to know: Where was God? We always expect that He should have intervened. But that's not the way it works. He gave us free will. I don't mean that in a pithy, dismissive way. His plan is profound, and it's why He doesn't generally stop tragic things from happening. But you know what else

He has done? He has called His people to stop doing evil to one another.

Not only are we meant to represent His image, but we are to represent His will. Jesus saved humanity by His own horrific suffering (yes, your God has suffered more than you), and He ascended to the right hand of God in heaven. But before He ascended, He gathered His disciples to give them the Great Commission to go into all the world and make disciples of all nations. He still had work to do, but after the resurrection of His Body, the Church picked up the responsibility for carrying out His work. When we serve Him by serving others and pointing to His presence, we continue Jesus' ministry to the dying world. We are His hands, feet, mouth, and to the degree we are abiding in Him, His mind.

We hope to do two things with this book: First, we hope to show you that God has always been there. He is present everywhere and always. God is not a God who looks away. As you read the rest of our story and its hardships, you need to know that God has always been with us, every step of the way. And as you look back at your own story and hardships, know that God has been right by your side, loving you, grieving with you, and ready to heal you from the wounds you have suffered. If He could jump in and take control of people without their permission and still somehow allow freedom and true loving between Himself and His people, He would do that, but that is not possible.

Our second goal is to be used by God to commission you to be one who points out His presence to the world, first by pointing out His presence in your life, and then by pointing to His presence in the lives of others.

> *Surely the presence of the Lord is in this place,*
> *I can feel His mighty power and His grace.*
> *I can hear the brush of angel's wings.*
> *I see glory on each face;*
> *Surely the presence of the Lord is in this place.*
> *In the midst of His children, the Lord said He would be.*
> *It doesn't take very many, it can be just two or three.*

And I feel the same sweet Spirit that I've felt oft times
*   before.*
Oh, surely I can say I have been with the Lord.
There's a holy hush around us as God's glory fills this
*   place.*
I've touched the hem of his garment and I can almost see
*   His face.*
And my heart is overflowing with the fullness of His joy.
I know without a doubt that I have been with the Lord.

— LANNY WOLFE 1977

Genesis 28:16 says, "Then Jacob awoke from his sleep and said, 'Surely the Lord is in this place, and I did not know it.'"

Matthew 18:20 says, "'For where two or three are gathered in my name, there am I among them.'"

God lives and dwells among us, and for the believer, He even dwells in us. But to take advantage of that fact, we must acknowledge Him and be mindful to "walk by the Spirit" (Galatians 5:16). We must be like Moses and the Israelites who, in one of their more noble moments, told the Lord, "If your Presence does not go with us, do not send us up from here" (Exodus 33:15 NIV).

God promises to be with us. He is always there, and if we will look to Him, He will guide us, comfort us, and help us no matter what we go through because we live in a fallen world that, while destined for perfection, is now far from it. We can always know that God is with us and live assuredly in the already-arriving Kingdom of His presence, His will done, and His goodness to us.

CHAPTER 3

HE PROMISES THE LOVE OF A FATHER THROUGH OUR ADOPTION

Adoption is more than a concept in Scripture—it's the heartbeat of the Gospel. In His infinite mercy, God doesn't just rescue us from sin; He makes us His children. Through Christ, He adopts us into His family, calls us sons and daughters, and grants us an eternal inheritance. This divine adoption is at the core of who we are as believers. We are offered a new identity and a relationship with our heavenly Father.

But adoption—whether heavenly or earthly—is not without pain. It requires sacrifice, patience, and the willingness to enter into brokenness. Yet, it is one of the most beautiful concepts that reflect God's love. In this chapter, we'll explore the depth of God's promise of adoption, how it has transformed our lives, and the personal journey of welcoming children into our home.

THE AWE-INSPIRING REALITY OF DIVINE ADOPTION

God's adoption of us is one of the most profound and awe-inspiring truths in all of Scripture. It is a promise that transforms our standing before Him, turning us from sinners into sons and daughters. J.I. Packer writes in his classic work *Knowing God*:

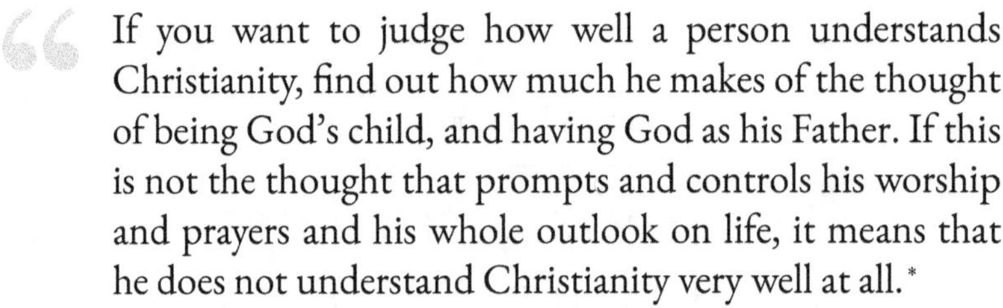

> If you want to judge how well a person understands Christianity, find out how much he makes of the thought of being God's child, and having God as his Father. If this is not the thought that prompts and controls his worship and prayers and his whole outlook on life, it means that he does not understand Christianity very well at all.*

Packer's words challenge us to consider the depth of what it means to be God's child. Adoption isn't just a title—it's an entirely new identity. As the Apostle Paul says in Romans 8:15-17 (NIV):

> The Spirit you received does not make you slaves, so that you live in fear again; rather, the Spirit you received brought about your adoption to sonship. And by Him we cry, *"Abba*, Father." The Spirit Himself testifies with our spirit that we are God's children. Now if we are children, then we are heirs—heirs of God and co-heirs with Christ.

This truth is staggering. We are no longer slaves to sin or fear; we are heirs of God and co-heirs with Christ! Consider the implications: Everything that belongs to Jesus is now ours. We are given access to the Father's throne, His promises, and His eternal home.

The King of Kings and Lord of Lords calls us His own. He is not distant or detached. He is a Father who delights in us, walks with us, and promises never to abandon us.

————

* J.I. Packer, *Knowing God*. InterVarsity Press, 2023.

Adoption as God's Promise

Paul writes in Galatians 4:4-6:

> But when the fullness of time had come, God sent forth his Son...to redeem those who were under the law, so that we might receive adoption as sons. And because you are sons, God has sent the Spirit of his Son into our hearts, crying, "Abba! Father!"

This passage reveals the profound reality of our adoption. God doesn't simply tolerate us—He chooses us. He brings us into His family and transforms our identity. Through adoption, we receive the Spirit of Christ, enabling us to call God "Abba," an intimate term akin to "Daddy."

Adoption is more than a legal transaction; it is an act of the heart. God demonstrates this by offering us unconditional love, belonging, and hope. Just as He adopts us into His family, He calls us to reflect this love to others by welcoming the orphaned and vulnerable.

The Start of Our Adoption Journey

Cindy and I never imagined adoption would be part of our story. Like many couples, we dreamed of having biological children and raising a family. But after years of trying and a devastating miscarriage, we found ourselves grieving deeply. It was during this time of loss that God began to redirect our hearts.

One day in 1998, Cindy heard a radio ad for the Bair Foundation, a Christian fostering agency. When I came home that evening, she was practically glowing with excitement. She had already gathered all the information and prepared a special dinner to share her vision with me. I'll admit, I was hesitant at first. But as we prayed together, God softened my heart, and we took the leap into fostering.

The process to become foster parents was overwhelming—fifty hours of training, home studies, and mountains of paperwork. I remember one night, as we filled out yet another form, Cindy looked at me and said, "Do you think God feels this way with us? Going through every detail of our lives, preparing a place for us in His family?" That thought carried us through the challenges ahead.

JOYS AND SORROWS OF FOSTERING

Our first placement was three brothers—ages four, six, and twelve. They arrived with a mix of excitement, fear, and pain. The youngest was a ball of energy, racing from room to room. The middle child was shy and withdrawn, while the eldest carried the weight of years of instability and rejection. Sudden parenthood was overwhelming, but also sacred. These boys needed love, and we were determined to give it.

Fostering brought immense joy and deep sorrow. The hardest moment of our journey came when our six-year-old foster son died in a tragic accident. He had only been with us for a few months, but we loved him as our own. The grief of his death was unimaginable. To make matters worse, we faced a lawsuit from his biological mother, who blamed us for his death. The media painted us as villains, twisting the story to fit a sensational narrative.

Through it all, we clung to God's promise of adoption. Just as He chose us despite our brokenness, we were called to love these children— even when it hurt. His faithfulness sustained us, and His example of sacrificial love gave us strength to keep going.

PHOEBE: THE MIRACLE WE DIDN'T EXPECT

In the midst of our grief, God brought us another foster child, Phoebe. She was born premature and was addicted to heroin and methamphetamine because of her mother's drug use. When we first held her tiny, trembling body, we knew she was a gift from God. We understood the road ahead would be hard—she spent her first month withdrawing from the drugs, crying in pain, and unable to sleep unless we held her tightly. As we cared for her, we saw God's grace at work.

Phoebe grew stronger, and our love for her deepened. Adopting her wasn't just a legal process; it was a spiritual calling. Every sleepless night and every tear shed was a reminder of the sacrifice God made to adopt us as His children.

Reflecting God's Love

Adoption is one of the most profound ways we can reflect the heart of God. It requires entering into brokenness and shouldering the burdens of another. Even though it's not easy, it is worth it. We encourage you to believe that every child who comes into your home brings with them the image of God and the opportunity for you to show them His unconditional love.

James 1:27 (NIV) reminds us: "Religion that God our Father accepts as pure and faultless is this: to look after orphans and widows in their distress..."

When we care for orphans, we participate in God's redemptive work. We become His hands and feet, offering hope to the hopeless and restoring what has been lost.

Encouragement for the Journey

If God is calling you to foster or adopt, know this: You don't have to be perfect. God doesn't call the equipped—He equips the called. He will provide the strength, wisdom, and grace you need for the journey.

If fostering or adopting isn't your calling, there are still countless ways to reflect the Father's heart for adoption. Pray for families who are fostering. Offer practical help like babysitting or meal delivery. Support organizations that care for orphans and vulnerable children. Every act of love matters.

The Love of a Father

Adoption is God's promise to us—a promise that we are chosen, loved, and secure in His family. It's a reflection of His heart and a call to share that love with others.

Tim Keller once said:

The only person who dares wake up a king at 3:00 a.m. for a glass of water is a child. We have that kind of access.[*]

This is the love of our Father. Just as He brought us into His family, may we open our hearts and homes to those who need His love. Together, we can participate in the redemptive work of our heavenly Father.

---

[*] Timothy Keller, Facebook post, 3 December 2019, "The only person who dares wake up a king at 3:00 AM for a glass of water is a child. We have that kind of access." https://www.facebook.com/TimKellerNYC/posts/the-only-person-who-dares-wake-up-a-king-at-300-am-for-a-glass-of-water-is-a-chi/2799625540077314/

CHAPTER 4

He Promises Faithfulness to His Bride

God's faithfulness to His people, often described as His "bride," offers a profound picture of unwavering love. This covenant love is central to both our faith and our marriages. From the beginning of time, God has demonstrated His commitment to His people, even when they failed Him. Marriage, as designed by God, is intended to reflect this divine love—a love that is sacrificial, enduring, and redemptive.

When Cindy and I said "I do," we had no idea the challenges we would face or the depths of God's faithfulness we would need to lean on. Through trials, heartbreak, and moments of joy, we discovered that faithfulness isn't just a feeling or a promise—it's a choice to love as God loves.

The Sacred Covenant of Marriage

Marriage, as described in Genesis 2:24, is not merely a partnership but a profound covenant: "...A man shall leave his father and his mother and hold fast to his wife, and they shall become one flesh." This "one flesh" union is more than physical; it's spiritual, emotional, and symbolic of God's relationship with His people.

Paul elaborates on this in Ephesians 5:25-27: "Husbands, love your wives, as Christ loved the church and gave himself up for her." Christ's sacrificial love for the Church is the gold standard for how husbands are called to love their wives. It's not about convenience or personal gain—it's about selfless devotion, even when it's costly.

Cindy and I learned this lesson the hard way. Our marriage wasn't always easy, and there were seasons when it felt like it might crumble under the weight of addiction, illness, and disappointment. But every time we were in a bad place, we turned to Scripture, and were reminded that marriage is meant to be a reflection of God's unwavering covenant with us. It's a promise that says, "I'm with you, no matter what."

A powerful illustration of this kind of covenant love can be seen in the movie *The Notebook*.* In the film, Noah spends years caring for Allie as she battles Alzheimer's, even when she no longer remembers him. His faithfulness is a testament to love that endures beyond circumstances or recognition. While their love story is fictional, it resonates because it mirrors the kind of love God has for us—one that never gives up, even when the other person can't reciprocate.

PRACTICAL WAYS TO CULTIVATE FAITHFULNESS IN MARRIAGE

Faithfulness doesn't happen by accident. It requires daily intentionality, a reliance on God, and a commitment to persevere through trials. Here are some expanded truths Cindy and I have learned that help us cultivate faithfulness in our marriage.

REMEMBER WHO THE REAL ENEMY IS

The turning point in our marriage came during a marriage conference when we heard the phrase, "Your spouse is not the enemy—Satan is." That truth revolutionized how we handled conflict. Before that, we often found ourselves fighting against each other, blaming and accusing. But when we realized that our real enemy was Satan, everything

---

* *The Notebook*, directed by Nick Cassavetes. Gran Via, 2004.

changed. Instead of tearing each other down, we began praying together, asking God to protect our marriage from division.

One night, during one of our darkest seasons, we had an argument that felt insurmountable. I went to the living room, ready to give up, but then the words from that conference echoed in my mind. I prayed aloud, "God, help me fight the real enemy here. Don't let Satan win." That prayer broke something in me. I went back to Cindy, and instead of arguing, I apologized. It was a small step, but it marked a shift in how we approached our struggles.

Root Your Marriage in God's Word

God's Word is the foundation of a strong marriage. During our hardest times, Cindy and I clung to verses like 1 Corinthians 13:4-5, NIV: "Love is patient, love is kind...it keeps no record of wrongs." This passage became our guide for how to love each other, even when it was difficult.

Early in our marriage, we decided to make Scripture reading a daily habit. On one occasion, we were reading Psalm 23 together, and the words "He restores my soul" struck us both. We realized that our marriage needed restoration, and we asked God to be the Shepherd of our relationship. From that day on, we saw His hand guiding us in ways we couldn't have imagined.

Keep Communication Open and Honest

Miscommunication can create cracks in even the strongest marriages. Cindy and I learned this the hard way during her battle with addiction. I often assumed I knew what she was feeling, and she assumed the same about me. It wasn't until we started having honest conversations—sometimes painful ones—that we began to understand each other better.

One practical step we took was scheduling regular "check-ins" where we'd sit down and ask, "How are you really doing?" These conversations helped us reconnect and address issues before they spiraled out of control.

PRAY TOGETHER DAILY

Prayer is the glue that holds a marriage together. When Cindy and I started praying together consistently, it changed the atmosphere of our home. One night, after a particularly hard day, we knelt by our bed and prayed for each other out loud. Hearing Cindy pray for me softened my heart in a way nothing else could.

If you're not praying together, start small. Begin with a short prayer before meals or bedtime, and let it grow naturally. Over time, those moments will become a lifeline for your relationship.

A GOD WHO NEVER ABANDONS HIS BRIDE

God's faithfulness to His people is the ultimate example of covenant love. Throughout Scripture, we see His relentless pursuit of His bride, even when she strays. Remember in Hosea when God called the prophet to marry a woman who would be unfaithful, as a symbol of His own unending love for Israel? In Ephesians, Paul reminds us that Christ loved the Church so much He gave His life for her.

This is the kind of faithfulness God calls us to emulate in marriage. It's not always easy. There were times when I wanted to give up on Cindy, when her addiction and depression felt like too much to bear. But God whispered to my heart, "I never gave up on you. Don't give up on her." That reminder carried me through some of the hardest moments of our marriage.

LOOKING AHEAD: GOD'S FORGIVENESS IN OUR FAILURES

Faithfulness in marriage is a reflection of God's faithfulness to us, but it's also a reminder of our need for His grace. We all fail—sometimes in small ways, sometimes in devastating ones. The next chapter will explore how God's forgiveness meets us in our lowest moments, especially when suffering leads us to sin. His grace is always greater than our failures, and His love is the foundation for healing and restoration. Join me as we dive deeper into the heart of God's forgiveness and its power to transform our lives.

Chapter 5

He Promises Forgiveness When Our Suffering Causes Us to Sin

Suffering is one of life's greatest tests. It stretches us, exposes us, and reveals parts of our character we'd rather keep hidden. Going through trials can drive us closer to God or cause us to spiral into sin. We may lash out in anger, grow bitter, or seek comfort in all the wrong places, and yet, even in our darkest moments, God's promise remains: He forgives us when we sin, even when our suffering is at the root of it.

This truth is a lifeline. As 1 John 1:9 reminds us: "If we confess our sins, he is faithful and just to forgive us our sins and to cleanse us from all unrighteousness." Hebrews 8:12 echoes this: "For I will be merciful toward their iniquities, and I will remember their sins no more."

God's forgiveness is not conditional on our behavior. Whether we sin out of rebellion or weakness, out of pride or pain, He stands ready to forgive us when we repent. This is the beauty of the Gospel: God meets us where we are, offering grace even when we feel most unworthy.

When Suffering Leads to Sin

In our story, Cindy's battle with chronic pain and opiate addiction brought turmoil into our home. The medications intended to relieve her suffering began to alter her personality. She became short-tempered and irritable, lashing out at Phoebe and me in ways that were deeply hurtful.

At the time, I didn't understand the full extent of the opiates' impact, and my responses were far from perfect. I grew angry, frustrated, and distant. Instead of turning to God for strength, I tried to manage everything on my own. Cindy, meanwhile, was trapped in a cycle of pain and addiction that clouded her judgment and strained her relationships.

Looking back, I see how suffering led us both to sin. Cindy's pain pushed her toward destructive behaviors, while my frustration drove me toward resentment and withdrawal. But even in that mess, God's forgiveness was at work. He didn't wait for us to fix ourselves or get it right. Instead, He extended grace in the midst of our brokenness and began the work of healing in our hearts.

God's Forgiveness in Scripture

The Bible is filled with stories of people who sinned in their suffering and yet found mercy in God's arms. The Israelites, for instance, had just witnessed God's miraculous power delivering them from Egypt when they began to complain and rebel. In Exodus 32, while Moses was on Mount Sinai, they made a golden calf to worship, driven by fear and impatience.

Despite their blatant idolatry, God forgave them after Moses interceded on their behalf. This story is a profound reminder that God's forgiveness is not limited by the severity of our sin. No matter how far we've fallen, He is always willing to restore us.

David's story offers another powerful example. After his grievous sins involving Bathsheba and Uriah, David turned to God in repentance, pouring out his heart in Psalm 51. Though his actions had dire consequences, God forgave him and continued to use him for His purposes.

These stories remind us that God's forgiveness is not only an act of grace but also a reflection of His unchanging character. As Psalm 103:14 says, "For he knows our frame; he remembers that we are dust."

THE ROLE OF REPENTANCE

While God's forgiveness is freely given, it requires us to acknowledge our sin and turn back to Him. Repentance is not about earning His grace—it's about receiving it. The story of the prodigal son in Luke 15 beautifully illustrates this truth.

When the prodigal son hit rock bottom, he realized the depth of his mistakes. He returned to his father, prepared to beg for forgiveness and accept the lowest position in the household. But his father had other plans. He ran to meet his son, embraced him, and celebrated his return with a feast.

This is the heart of repentance: admitting our need for God's mercy and trusting that He will forgive. It's not always easy. Admitting fault can feel like ripping open a wound. But when we bring our brokenness to God, He doesn't shame us. Instead, He heals us.

Cindy's journey through repentance was not linear or easy. Her Step Study with Celebrate Recovery forced her to confront years of pain and sin. As she worked through her inventory, painful memories surfaced, and those around her felt the ripple effects. But those were necessary steps in her healing. That process ultimately deepened her dependence on God's grace.

GOD'S PURPOSE IN SUFFERING

It's a hard truth, but sometimes God allows suffering to expose what's in our hearts. The Israelites' time in the wilderness was filled with tests: Would they trust God to provide, or would they grumble? Would they believe in His promises, or would they let fear rule them?

Tabletalk Magazine offers this insight:

> Sometimes God brings us into the wilderness to reveal the ugly truth about who we really are—even as those whom God has delivered from bondage. We are still

deeply sinful, unbelieving people who find faith a constant struggle.*

While this may be difficult to accept, suffering truly can be a gift. Suffering can either harden us or refine us, depending on how we respond. When we allow God to use our pain for His purposes, even difficult journeys become tools for growth and transformation.

HOW TO RECEIVE GOD'S FORGIVENESS

Receiving God's forgiveness is both simple and profound. It requires two things: admitting our sin and turning away from it. This process, called repentance, is at the heart of renewal. True repentance is not just about feeling sorry—it's about coming before God in humility, recognizing our need for His mercy, and allowing Him to cleanse and restore us.

David's prayer in Psalm 51 is one of the clearest examples of genuine repentance. In these verses, we see him crying out to God—not just for forgiveness, but for transformation:

> Have mercy on me, O God,
>   according to your steadfast love;
> according to your abundant mercy
>   blot out my transgressions.
> Wash me thoroughly from my iniquity,
>   and cleanse me from my sin!
> For I know my transgressions,
>   and my sin is ever before me.
> Against you, you only, have I sinned
>   and done what is evil in your sight,
> so that you may be justified in your words
>   and blameless in your judgment.
> Behold, I was brought forth in iniquity,
>   and in sin did my mother conceive me.

---

* Iain Duguid, "Israel's Testing in the Wilderness." *Tabletalk*, August 2023 issue.

Behold, you delight in truth in the inward being,
  and you teach me wisdom in the secret heart.
Purge me with hyssop, and I shall be clean;
  wash me, and I shall be whiter than snow.
Let me hear joy and gladness;
  let the bones that you have broken rejoice.
Hide your face from my sins,
  and blot out all my iniquities.
Create in me a clean heart, O God,
  and renew a right[b] spirit within me.
Cast me not away from your presence,
  and take not your Holy Spirit from me.
Restore to me the joy of your salvation,
  and uphold me with a willing spirit.
Then I will teach transgressors your ways,
  and sinners will return to you.
Deliver me from bloodguiltiness, O God,
    O God of my salvation,
      and my tongue will sing aloud of your right-
eousness.

— PSALM 51:1-14

David's words give a clear picture of what it looks like to receive God's forgiveness and be restored. Here's how we can apply this to our lives:

1. Admit Your Sin

The first step in receiving God's forgiveness is acknowledging your sin before Him. David didn't make excuses or shift blame—he owned his failure completely. He said, "For I know my transgressions, and my sin is ever before me" (v. 3).

Repentance requires honesty. It means bringing our sin into the light, confessing it to God, and recognizing that we've fallen short. Sometimes, this step is painful, because it means facing the weight of what we've done. But the beauty of confession is that it opens the door to healing.

2. Turn Away from Sin

Repentance is more than just saying sorry—it's about changing direction. David didn't just ask for forgiveness; he pleaded for transformation. He cried out, "Create in me a clean heart, O God, and renew a right spirit within me" (v. 10).

True repentance leads to a change in behavior. When we turn from sin, we are actively choosing to walk in a different direction—toward God's ways instead of our own.

This doesn't mean we won't struggle. Old temptations will still surface. But when we continually seek God and surrender to His Spirit, He strengthens us to resist sin and walk in righteousness.

3. Receive God's Grace

One of the hardest things for many people is to truly accept God's forgiveness. We often carry guilt long after we've repented, thinking we need to "make it up to God" before we can move forward. But that's not how grace works.

David trusted in God's mercy: "Restore to me the joy of your salvation, and uphold me with a willing spirit" (v. 12).

Forgiveness is not about what we do—it's about what Christ has already done for us on the cross. When we confess, repent, and receive God's grace, we can walk in the joy of salvation, knowing that our sins have been completely washed away.

The Power of God's Forgiveness

God's forgiveness is life-changing. It's not just about wiping away our past mistakes—it's about restoring our hearts, giving us a fresh start, and leading us into a life of freedom.

David understood this well. After repenting, he didn't stay stuck in shame. Instead, he declared, "Then I will teach transgressors your ways, and sinners will return to you" (v. 13). His experience of grace became a testimony to others.

That's what happens when we receive God's forgiveness. We don't just get a second chance—we get a transformed heart. With that transformation comes the ability to extend grace to others and testify to God's goodness.

If you're carrying guilt, shame, or regret today, God invites you to receive His mercy. No sin is too great, no failure too deep—His grace is greater. Come before Him, confess, turn away from sin, and receive the joy of His salvation.

How to Sin Less in Suffering

Of course, the goal is not just to seek forgiveness after we sin, but to honor God in our suffering and sin less in the first place. This is no easy task, but with God's help, it is possible.

The Apostle Paul provides a powerful example. In 2 Corinthians 6:3-10, he describes how he and fellow servants of God endured afflictions, hardships, and even beatings with purity, patience, and kindness. Their suffering became a testament to God's power and faithfulness.

To sin less in suffering, we must first understand that God uses our pain to refine us. Just as fire purifies gold, trials can shape us into Christ's likeness if we allow them. This doesn't mean we seek out suffering, but when it comes, we trust that it has a purpose.

Second, we must rely on God's strength. When temptation feels overwhelming, we can cling to the promise of 1 Corinthians 10:13: "God is faithful, and he will not let you be tempted beyond your ability, but with the temptation he will also provide the way of escape..."

Finally, we must fix our eyes on Jesus. He endured the ultimate suffering on our behalf, and His example gives us both hope and direction. As Hebrews 12:1b-2a says: "Let us run with endurance the race that is set before us, looking to Jesus, the founder and perfecter of our faith."

EXTENDING FORGIVENESS TO OTHERS

God's forgiveness is not just something we receive—it's something we are called to extend to others. This can be one of the most difficult commands in Scripture, especially when suffering has come at the hands of another person. Whether it's betrayal, abuse, neglect, or even just the pain of unmet expectations, holding onto bitterness can feel justified. But as followers of Christ, we are called to a higher standard.

1. The Command to Forgive

Forgiveness is not optional for believers. It's not something we extend only when we feel like it or when we think someone deserves it. Jesus makes this clear in Matthew 6:14-15:

> For if you forgive others their trespasses, your heavenly Father will also forgive you, but if you do not forgive others their trespasses, neither will your Father forgive your trespasses.

This teaching is hard. It reminds us that forgiveness is not just about the person who hurt us—it's about our relationship with God. Unforgiveness creates a barrier between us and the Lord, not because He withholds His love, but because bitterness hardens our hearts.

Paul echoes this in Colossians 3:13: "Bear with each other and forgive one another, if any of you has a grievance against someone. Forgive as the Lord forgave you" (NIV).

When we struggle to forgive, we must remember the depth of our own sin and the extravagant grace God has shown us. None of us deserve forgiveness, yet Christ freely gives it.

2. The Cost of Unforgiveness

Many people think that holding onto resentment gives them power— that it somehow protects them from being hurt again. But the reality is, unforgiveness only chains us to the past. It keeps wounds open, allowing them to fester rather than heal.

Jesus illustrated this in Matthew 18:21-35 in the parable of the unforgiving servant. In the story, a servant is forgiven a massive debt by his master. But instead of extending the same mercy, the servant demands payment from another servant who owes him a small amount. When the master finds out, he is outraged and throws the first servant into prison.

Jesus ends the parable with this warning: "So also my heavenly Father will do to every one of you, if you do not forgive your brother from your heart" (Matthew 18:35).

Unforgiveness is a prison. It binds us in anger, resentment, and pain. Studies have even shown that bitterness can have physical consequences—high blood pressure, stress, anxiety, and depression. God commands us to forgive not just for the sake of others, but for our own freedom.

3. What Forgiveness Is (and What It Isn't)

One of the biggest struggles people have with forgiveness is misunderstanding what it actually means. Here's some clarity: Forgiveness is not excusing the wrong. It does not mean saying, "It's okay" when it's not. Sin is never okay, and God does not overlook it.

Forgiveness is not forgetting. The phrase "forgive and forget" is not biblical. Some wounds run deep, and memories linger. But forgiveness means we choose not to let those memories control us.

Forgiveness is also not allowing continued abuse. If someone has harmed you, forgiving them does not mean allowing them to continue hurting you. Boundaries are important. Forgiveness and reconciliation are not always the same thing.

Forgiveness is a choice, not a feeling. You may not feel like forgiving, but obedience to God is not based on feelings. It is an act of faith.

4. How to Forgive

So how do we actually forgive when everything in us resists? Here are some biblical steps:

Step 1: Acknowledge the Hurt

Before we can truly forgive, we must be honest about our pain. Some people try to rush past this step, thinking it's more "Christian" to just move on. But God never asks us to ignore our wounds. Even Jesus, on the cross, acknowledged the pain inflicted upon Him when He prayed, "Father, forgive them, for they know not what they do" (Luke 23:34a).

Take time to grieve the hurt. Bring it to God in prayer. Tell Him how deeply it has affected you.

Step 2: Recognize How Much You've Been Forgiven

When we struggle to forgive, it's often because we have lost sight of how much we ourselves have been forgiven. In Luke 7:47, Jesus says: "Therefore I tell you, her sins, which are many, are forgiven—for she loved much. But he who is forgiven little, loves little."

Of course, none of us are "forgiven little." We have all been forgiven an unpayable debt. When we remember this, it softens our hearts toward others.

Step 3: Choose to Forgive

Forgiveness is a choice. You may not feel it right away, but you must decide to release the offender to God. Say it out loud if you have to:

"God, I choose to forgive ____. I release them from the debt they owe me. I entrust this situation to You, knowing You are just and good."

Step 4: Pray for the Person Who Hurt You

This may be the hardest step, but Jesus commands it: "But I say to you, Love your enemies and pray for those who persecute you" (Matthew 5:44).

Praying for the person who wronged you does not mean you have to be relationally close to them. It does not mean trusting them again if they have broken your trust. But it does mean surrendering your heart to God and asking Him to work in the lives of both of you.

Step 5: Keep Choosing Forgiveness

Forgiveness is not a one-time event. Feelings of anger or pain may resurface, and when they do, you must choose again to forgive. Jesus told Peter to forgive "seventy times seven" times (Matthew 18:22 NLT), meaning to forgive without limit.

5. The Power of Forgiveness

When we forgive, something incredible happens—we break free. We step out of the chains of bitterness and into the peace of God. We reflect Jesus to the world, showing His love in action. Sometimes, forgiveness does lead to healing and reconciliation.

Corrie ten Boom, a survivor of the Holocaust, tells a powerful story of forgiveness. After the war, she encountered a former Nazi guard from the concentration camp where she had suffered. The man, now a Christian, asked for her forgiveness. She describes how, in that moment, she did not feel capable of forgiving—but as she prayed, God's love flooded her heart, and she extended her hand in forgiveness.

She later wrote: "To forgive is to set a prisoner free and to discover that the prisoner was you."[*]

Forgiveness is one of the greatest gifts we can give—not just to others, but to ourselves.

6. A Final Word: Forgiving Yourself

Sometimes, the hardest person to forgive is yourself. If you are carrying guilt over past mistakes, hear this: God has already forgiven you. 1 John 1:9 declares: "If we confess our sins, he is faithful and just to forgive us our sins and to cleanse us from all unrighteousness."

If God, in His perfect holiness, does not hold your past against you, then who are you to hold onto it? Let go. Receive His grace. Walk in the freedom of His forgiveness.

As we move forward in this book, let's explore what it means to

---

[*] Corrie ten Boom, *The Hiding Place*. Baker Publishing Group, 2006, page 247.

truly live in that freedom—the joy of knowing we are forgiven and extending that forgiveness to others. In the next chapter, we'll consider the glorious news that our suffering, no matter how severe, has an end date.

CHAPTER 6

HE PROMISES TO RETURN AND END OUR SUFFERING

In Part Two, we will explore God's gifts to those who suffer, but first, we must close Part One with the best promise of all: God has promised to return and bring an end to suffering forever. This is not just a theological idea or a comforting thought—it is a hope rooted in the very character and faithfulness of God. It's a promise that fuels our endurance, strengthens our faith, and gives purpose to even the darkest seasons of our lives.

As we live our lives, questions inevitably arise—questions so deep and painful that only God Himself could answer them. Why do the innocent suffer? Why do children die? Why does God allow evil to persist? These are questions that many of us have wrestled with, and they often remain unanswered on this side of eternity. But the Bible gives us a glimpse of a future where these questions may not matter anymore, because sorrow will cease, and joy will overflow. Revelation 21:4 assures us of this, saying,

> He will wipe away every tear from their eyes, and death shall be no more, neither shall there be mourning, nor crying, nor pain anymore, for the former things have passed away.

This promise is at the heart of the Christian faith: the hope of restoration. When we focus on this hope, it transforms how we endure suffering. It gives us a lens through which we can view our trials—not as meaningless pain, but as a refining process that draws us closer to God and prepares us for eternal joy.

The Day Everything Changed

September 19, 2010 began like any other day. As usual, Cindy home-schooled Phoebe and cared for our ten-month-old grand-daughter, Miriam. We had taken Miriam in because her mother, Mary, was unable to care for her due to her own struggles. Miriam had become a source of joy and comfort for us in a season filled with pain. But that evening, everything changed.

Around 10:00 p.m., we received a call that Mary had been in a terrible accident and was being rushed to the hospital. We quickly dressed, left Miriam at home with Phoebe, and drove to the emergency room. The scene that greeted us was chaotic. At first, the hospital staff wouldn't even let us see Mary because she had been mistakenly checked in under someone else's name. Cindy, desperate and determined, caused enough of a scene that a police officer intervened and verified our identities. Finally, we were allowed into Mary's room.

What we saw was a nightmare. Mary was unconscious and hooked up to machines as doctors worked frantically to stabilize her. Memories of losing our foster son in 1999 flooded my mind. I held Cindy's hand as we prayed for a miracle, but deep down, I feared the worst. At one point, Cindy spoke to Mary, and though she couldn't respond, a single tear slid down her cheek. It was a small sign that she could hear us, and we clung to it with fragile hope.

Around 2:00 a.m., Mary was moved to the ICU. We waited in the family room, exhausted and terrified. Then we heard it: "Code blue, ICU." We knew it was her. Minutes stretched into eternity as we waited for an update. When the nurse finally brought us back to Mary's room, it was clear the situation was dire. For forty agonizing minutes, the medical team tried to revive her, but eventually, they had to call it. Mary was gone.

WRESTLING WITH THE "WHY"

Losing Mary was devastating. She wasn't just our daughter; she was a young mother, and her loss meant that Miriam would never know her biological mom. The grief was compounded by financial stress as we struggled to cover funeral costs. We wanted to honor Mary's wish to be buried, but the expense was overwhelming. With the help of our church community, we were able to raise some funds, but ultimately, we had to choose cremation. It broke our hearts, but we had no other option.

In the days and weeks that followed, I found myself asking God, "Why?" Why had we endured so much loss? Why had our family been touched by so much tragedy? People often say, "God won't give you more than you can handle," but that's a misquote of scripture. The truth is, life often gives us more than we can handle on our own. That's why we need God.

Through this season, I learned that God doesn't always give us answers, but He always gives us Himself. As I poured out my pain to Him, I began to see that our suffering wasn't wasted. God was using it to shape us, to refine us, and to prepare us for something greater. "For I consider that the sufferings of this present time are not worth comparing with the glory that is to be revealed to us" (Romans 8:18).

THE TENSION OF PRESENT PAIN AND FUTURE GLORY

Suffering often forces us into one of two extremes: living entirely in the pain of the present or escaping entirely into the hope of the future. Both responses are understandable, but neither fully captures the balance God desires for us. We are called to live in the tension—acknowledging our pain while anchoring our hope in Christ's return.

When Cindy experienced medically-induced depression as a side effect of her pain medication, it thrust us into one of the darkest seasons of our lives. Her physical suffering was unbearable, but the emotional toll was even greater. Depression clouded her mind, leading to suicidal thoughts and despair so deep that I wasn't sure she would survive. I vividly remember the night I had to rush her to the emergency room, only to hear the doctors recommend admitting her to a psychiatric facility.

This was uncharted territory for us. While we were familiar with psychiatric care because of our son Jacob's struggles, this was the first time Cindy herself had to walk through that valley. Watching her endure this was heartbreaking. I couldn't fix it. I couldn't pray it away. All I could do was hold onto the promise that God was with us, even in the darkness. "The Lord is near to the brokenhearted and saves the crushed in spirit" (Psalm 34:18).

The Hope of Christ's Return

Why does all of this matter? Because Christ has promised to return and set everything right. This promise is not just a future hope; it is a present anchor. Revelation 22:12 says, "Behold, I am coming soon, bringing my recompense with me, to repay each one for what he has done."

This is not just a promise of judgment; it is a promise of restoration. Every wrong will be made right. Every tear will be wiped away. Every wound will be healed. For those who have trusted in Christ, the return of Jesus means the end of all suffering and the beginning of eternal joy.

Paul captures this beautifully in his letter to the Romans:

> For the creation waits with eager longing for the revealing of the sons of God. For the creation was subjected to futility...in hope that the creation itself will be set free from its bondage to corruption and obtain the freedom of the glory of the children of God.
>
> — Romans 8:19-21

Not only do we long for redemption, but all of creation does as well. When Adam sinned, the world was plunged into brokenness, but Christ's return will usher in a new creation—a world free from pain, sin, and death.

LIVING IN LIGHT OF HIS PROMISE

What does it mean to live in light of Christ's return? It means living with a hope that transforms every aspect of our lives, even in the face of suffering and loss. The apostle Paul reminds us that we do not "grieve as others do who have no hope" (1 Thessalonians 4:13b). This doesn't mean we don't grieve at all—grief is a natural response to the brokenness of the world—but it does mean that our grief is anchored in hope. Our sorrow is not despair, because we know that God has the final word.

Living in light of His promises means recognizing that the pain and struggles of this life are not the end of the story. Suffering, though real and often overwhelming, is temporary. It is a chapter, not the whole book. Paul captures this truth in 2 Corinthians 4:17: "For this light momentary affliction is preparing for us an eternal weight of glory beyond all comparison." Notice that Paul calls our affliction "light" and "momentary." This doesn't minimize the reality of our pain—it elevates the reality of the glory to come. The eternal joy and restoration awaiting us are so profound, so magnificent, that they will make even the heaviest burdens seem light by comparison.

This shift in perspective changes everything. It allows us to endure trials with perseverance, to face loss with courage, and to invest our lives in things that truly matter. Living in light of Christ's return means fixing our eyes on the eternal rather than being consumed by the temporary. It means asking ourselves hard but necessary questions: What am I building my life on? Am I striving for things that will pass away, or am I living for things that will last forever?

C.S. Lewis captures this beautifully in The Chronicles of Narnia when he writes:

> *Wrong will be right, when Aslan comes in sight,*
> *At the sound of his roar, sorrows will be no more,*
> *When he bares his teeth, winter meets its death,*

*And when he shakes his mane, we shall have spring
again.*[*]

This poetic image of Aslan's return points us to the far greater reality of Christ's return. Just as Aslan's presence restores Narnia, Christ's return will restore our broken world. Every injustice will be set right. Every sorrow will be turned into joy. Every tear will be wiped away. This is not wishful thinking; it is the unshakable promise of God.

What Does This Look Like in Daily Life?

Living in light of His promise means allowing this hope to shape our actions, our priorities, and our relationships. It means refusing to let fear, despair, or bitterness take root in our hearts, because we know that redemption is on the horizon. Here are practical ways this hope manifests in our lives:

1. Persevering Through Trials

When we face hardship, we can endure with the knowledge that our suffering is not meaningless. God is using it to shape us, refine us, and prepare us for eternity. James writes,

> Blessed is the one who perseveres under trial because, having stood the test, that person will receive the crown of life that the Lord has promised to those who love him.
>
> — James 1:12 NIV

Every trial we endure with faith becomes a testimony to God's sustaining grace and a building block in our eternal reward.

---

[*] C.S. Lewis, *The Lion, the Witch and the Wardrobe: Full Color Edition.* HarperCollins, 2000, page 79.

2. Investing in Eternal Things

Knowing that Christ will return changes how we use our time, energy, and resources. Instead of chasing after temporary pleasures or worldly success, we prioritize what will last forever: loving God, loving others, and advancing His kingdom. Jesus reminds us in Matthew 6:19-20a:

> Do not lay up for yourselves treasures on earth, where moth and rust destroy and where thieves break in and steal, but lay up for yourselves treasures in heaven.

Living for eternity gives us clarity about what truly matters.

3. Living with Purpose and Mission

Christ's promise to return motivates us to share the gospel with urgency. We want others to experience the same hope and redemption we have found in Him. As ambassadors of Christ, we are called to shine His light in a dark world, knowing that our labor is not in vain.

> Therefore, my dear brothers and sisters, stand firm. Let nothing move you. Always give yourselves fully to the work of the Lord, because you know that your labor in the Lord is not in vain.

> — 1 CORINTHIANS 15:58 NIV

4. Loving Others Well

Living in light of Christ's return changes how we view our relationships. We see others not as obstacles or inconveniences but as eternal souls created in the image of God. This compels us to love sacrificially, forgive generously, and serve selflessly. As Paul writes, "Be kind to one another, tenderhearted, forgiving one another, as God in Christ forgave you" (Ephesians 4:32).

The Hope That Sustains Us

This hope is not just for the future—it sustains us here and now. It gives us the strength to keep going when the road is hard, the courage to face uncertainty, and the peace to rest in God's sovereignty. It reminds us that even when we don't understand the "why" of our suffering, we can trust the "who"—the God who loves us, walks with us, and promises to make all things new.

One of the most profound truths of the Christian faith is that we don't walk this journey alone. The Holy Spirit, whom Jesus calls the Comforter, is with us every step of the way.

> Likewise the Spirit helps us in our weakness. For we do not know what to pray for as we ought, but the Spirit himself intercedes for us with groanings too deep for words.
>
> — ROMANS 8:26

In our darkest moments, when words fail and hope seems distant, the Spirit intercedes on our behalf, reminding us that we are not abandoned.

Looking Toward the Future

The promise of Christ's return calls us to look beyond our present circumstances and fix our eyes on eternity. It reminds us that this world is not our home—we are pilgrims passing through, citizens of a heavenly kingdom. Hebrews 13:14 says, "For here we have no lasting city, but we seek the city that is to come." This perspective frees us from the need to cling tightly to the things of this world. It allows us to live with open hands, ready to give, serve, and sacrifice, because we know that our true reward is yet to come.

The apostle John paints a breathtaking picture of this future in Revelation 21:1, 3-4b (NIV):

 Then I saw "a new heaven and a new earth," for the first heaven and the first earth had passed away…And I heard a loud voice from the throne saying, "Look! God's dwelling place is now among the people, and he will dwell with them. They will be his people, and God himself will be with them and be their God. He will wipe every tear from their eyes. There will be no more death…"

This is our destiny as followers of Christ: to dwell with God in a world made new, free from sin, pain, and death. This is the hope we hold onto, the promise that sustains us through every trial and every sorrow.

HOLDING ONTO HOPE

Living in light of Christ's return doesn't mean we ignore the challenges of this life. Instead, it means we face them with a steadfast hope, knowing that our story doesn't end here. It means we endure with joy, persevere with faith, and love with abandon, because we know that the best is yet to come.

When the road is hard and the burden feels too heavy, remember the words of Jesus: "Yes, I am coming soon" (Revelation 22:20 NIV), and let the truth of His promise carry you forward, one step at a time, until the day we see Him face to face.

ENCOURAGEMENT FOR THE JOURNEY

If you are walking through a season of suffering, take heart: Your pain is not meaningless. Christ sees you, loves you, and is with you. His return is a guarantee that all things will be made new. In the meantime, He invites us to entrust our souls to Him, knowing that He is faithful (1 Peter 4:19).

As we close this chapter, let us remember the words of Revelation 21:5: "Behold, I am making all things new." This is the promise we cling to, the hope that sustains us, and the reason we can face tomorrow with courage.

PART TWO

GOD'S GIFTS TO THE SUFFERING

Chapter 7

—

He Gives Us the Suffering Savior

Life is unpredictable, and suffering often comes when we least expect it. For our family, one of those moments happened on an ordinary day—April 22nd—when Miriam decided to go outside to get the mail. It wasn't supposed to be a big deal. She had a package waiting and couldn't contain her excitement, so she begged to retrieve it herself. The neighborhood was under construction, with large trucks lining the streets and drivers who often ignored speed limits. The risk was always there, but like so many parents, we never thought such a simple task would result in heartbreak.

When Miriam stepped into the crosswalk, a construction van stopped to let her cross. But as she walked forward, another truck sped around the van, clipping her with its side mirror. The impact was brutal, collapsing her left cheekbone and giving her a major concussion. Though the driver stopped to check on her, the damage was done. I rushed to her, gathered information from the driver, and then Cindy and I raced to the emergency room, hearts pounding with fear.

The ER staff confirmed multiple facial fractures and the concussion. The injuries would require specialized care, but to our dismay, the hospital sent us home, advising us to wait and schedule surgery at Children's Hospital in Denver. When we finally saw the surgeon, he was frustrated with the delay. By then, Miriam's bones had already begun to heal incorrectly, making the procedure far more difficult than it should have been. What was supposed to be a two-hour surgery stretched to over four hours as the surgeon painstakingly worked to repair the damage.

It was yet another chapter in our family's ongoing saga of suffering—a story that often feels like more than we can bear. But through it all, we've learned to rely on the One who suffered for us, our Savior, who not only understands our pain but entered into it fully.

THE WEIGHT OF "MOTS"

In our family, the phrase "MOTS" (More of the Same) has become a way to describe the ongoing challenges we face. It's a term borrowed from a Denver weatherman who used it to signal days of unchanging weather patterns. For us, MOTS describes the steady rhythm of hardship, where one trial follows another, and we rarely have time to catch our breath before the next wave hits. Our normal is not what most families would consider normal, but it's the life we've been given.

We don't say this to complain. Instead, we've come to see these hardships as a way to align ourselves with the suffering Savior. As we face each new challenge, we're reminded that Jesus Himself walked a road of pain and sorrow, and through His example, we find strength. While we may not know when our earthly suffering will end, we cling to the promise that it will end—either when we are called home or when Christ returns. Until then, we hold fast to faith, hope, and the love of our Savior.

THE SUFFERING SAVIOR

Philip Yancey, in his book *Finding God in Unexpected Places*, reflects on the story of Job, a man whose suffering we've looked at earlier, but his suffering was so profound that I want to look at his life again. In the middle of his suffering, Job questioned whether God could truly understand his pain. In Job 10:4-5, Job asks:

> Have you eyes of flesh?
>   Do you see as man sees?
>   Are your days as the days of man,
>   or your years as a man's years,

In essence, Job was asking God, "Do you have any idea what it's like to be human? Do you know what it feels like to suffer?"

At the time, Job didn't know what we now know: God does understand. Jesus, the Lamb of God, is the suffering Savior who willingly stepped into our broken world to experience pain, loss, rejection, and even death. Through Christ, we have an answer to Job's question: Yes, God knows exactly what it's like to be here. He doesn't merely observe our suffering from a distance—He entered into it fully.

DOES HE STILL SUFFER?

One of the most comforting truths about Christ is that He not only suffered in the past but continues to share in our pain. As parents, we know the unique agony of watching our children suffer. It's a helpless, heart-wrenching feeling, and every loving parent would gladly trade places with their child to spare them pain. This is the kind of love Jesus has for us—a love that willingly bore the cross.

When Jesus approached Jerusalem in the week leading up to His death, He cried out:

> O Jerusalem, Jerusalem, the city that kills the prophets and stones those who are sent to it! How often would I have gathered your children together as a hen gathers her brood under her wings, and you were not willing!
>
> — MATTHEW 23:37

This lament reveals the heart of a suffering parent—a Savior who longed to protect His people but was rejected. His suffering didn't end with the cross. Even now, He grieves for those who reject His love and continues to intercede for us as we walk through our own trials.

Isaiah prophesied the suffering of Christ with vivid, heart-wrenching detail:

> He was despised and rejected by men,
> > a man of sorrows and acquainted with grief;
> and as one from whom men hide their faces
> > he was despised, and we esteemed him not.
> Surely he has borne our griefs
> > and carried our sorrows;
> yet we esteemed him stricken,
> > smitten by God, and afflicted.
> But he was pierced for our transgressions;
> > he was crushed for our iniquities;
> upon him was the chastisement that brought us peace,
> > and with his wounds we are healed.

> — ISAIAH 53:3-5

These words remind us that Jesus not only understands suffering but chose to endure it for our sake. His wounds became the means of our healing, and His sacrifice paved the way for our redemption.

FINDING PURPOSE IN SUFFERING

Suffering often feels like a cruel and meaningless interruption to life. When we're in the thick of pain, it's natural to ask, "Why is this happening? What good could possibly come from this?" But through Christ, we are invited to see suffering in a new light—not as a pointless burden, but as an opportunity to find purpose, healing, and even joy.

Paul touches on this profound truth in Colossians 1:24 when he writes:

> Now I rejoice in my sufferings for your sake, and in my flesh I am filling up what is lacking in Christ's afflictions for the sake of his body, that is, the church.

At first glance, this verse might seem perplexing, as if Paul were suggesting that Christ's suffering on the cross was incomplete or insufficient. But that's not what he means. Christ's sacrifice was perfect, final, and all-encompassing. There is nothing anyone could ever add to the atonement He achieved on the cross. Paul isn't saying that Christ's work needs supplementing; rather, he's revealing an incredible truth about how God uses our suffering as part of His redemptive plan.

SUFFERING AS A TESTIMONY

What Paul is pointing out is this: It often happens that through the suffering of believers, others come to experience and know the reality of the gospel. Christ's sacrifice reconciled us to God once and for all. The message of that sacrifice spreads to others through our lives—and often through our willingness to endure hardship for His sake. When we choose to trust God in the middle of our pain, when we choose faith over despair, our lives become a powerful testimony to His love, grace, and strength.

Suffering, then, isn't without meaning. In fact, it's one of the ways God displays His glory to the world. When people see us endure trials with hope and peace that don't make sense in human terms, it causes them to wonder, "What do they have that I don't?" Our suffering becomes a megaphone, proclaiming God's goodness and pointing others to Christ.

Think about your own suffering for a moment. What hardships have you faced? What pain have you endured? Now consider this: How might God use your experiences to point others to Him? It's not easy to examine our wounds for lessons, especially when the pain is still fresh, but it's an important task.

CHOOSING FAITH OVER BITTERNESS

When we endure suffering, we have a choice. We can allow bitterness and resentment to take root, turn inward, and close ourselves off from God. Or we can surrender our pain to Him, trusting that He will use it for good—even if we can't see how in the moment.

This choice is critical because bitterness poisons our hearts and isolates us from the very hope we need to endure. When we let bitterness take over, our suffering serves no purpose. It simply becomes an endless loop of pain and despair. But when we surrender our pain to God, something incredible happens. He takes what was meant for harm and transforms it into something beautiful and redemptive. He gives our suffering purpose, allowing it to bring hope and healing not only to us but to those around us.

Paul's life is a perfect example of this. He endured beatings, imprisonment, shipwrecks, hunger, and countless other hardships for the sake of the gospel. Yet, in all of it, he found joy—not because the suffering itself was pleasant, but because he knew it was being used for a greater purpose. Paul's suffering wasn't wasted; it became a tool in God's hands to spread the gospel and strengthen the church.

A DIVINE PERSPECTIVE ON SUFFERING

It's difficult to see the purpose of our suffering when we're in the middle of it. But Scripture reminds us that God's perspective is far greater than ours. Romans 8:28 assures us, "In all things God works for the good of those who love him, who have been called according to his purpose." This doesn't mean that all things are good—it means that God can bring good out of even the darkest circumstances.

Sometimes, the good that comes from our suffering is internal. God uses trials to refine our character, deepen our faith, and draw us closer to Him. Other times, the good is external. Our suffering becomes a platform for ministry, a way to encourage and uplift others who are walking through similar pain.

It's not easy to embrace this perspective. When the pain is raw, the last thing we want to think about is how God might use it. But as we surrender our pain to Him, He begins to reveal the ways He is working through it.

Suffering and the Gospel

There is a unique connection between suffering and the gospel. At its core, the gospel is a story of suffering—a story of a Savior who willingly endured the agony of the cross to bring redemption to a broken world. When we suffer, we have the opportunity to reflect that same sacrificial love to the people around us.

Paul touches on this connection in Philippians 3:10 when he says, "I want to know Christ—yes, to know the power of his resurrection and participation in his sufferings, becoming like him in his death" (NIV). This is a profound statement. Paul isn't just saying he wants to know Christ's power; he's saying he wants to share in Christ's sufferings. Why? Because it's in those moments of suffering that we become most like Him.

Jesus' suffering wasn't meaningless, and neither is ours. Just as His suffering brought redemption to the world, our suffering can bring light and hope to those who are lost in darkness.

A Living Testimony

Think about someone in your life who has faced unimaginable suffering yet continued to trust God. Their faith, even in the midst of pain, likely had a profound impact on you. Maybe their story inspired you to cling to God during your own trials. Maybe their endurance reminded you that God is faithful, even when life feels unbearable.

Now think about how your own story might impact others. What if your willingness to trust God in the middle of your suffering became the catalyst for someone else to encounter His love? What if your pain, surrendered to Him, became the very thing He used to draw someone else to Christ?

This is the paradox of suffering in the Christian life: What feels like a burden too heavy to bear can become a blessing when placed in God's hands. Our suffering doesn't diminish us; it refines us, strengthens us, and allows us to reflect His glory more clearly.

EMBRACING THE PURPOSE IN SUFFERING

Finding purpose in suffering doesn't mean we pretend the hard road is easy or enjoyable. It doesn't mean we minimize the pain or act as if it doesn't matter. Instead, it means we trust that God is at work, even when we can't see it. It means we cling to the hope that He will use our suffering for His glory and our good.

Paul's words in Colossians 1:24 are a powerful reminder that our suffering is never wasted. When we endure hardship with faith and trust, our lives become a living testimony to the sufficiency of Christ. Our pain, surrendered to Him, becomes a tool in His hands to bring hope, healing, and salvation to a hurting world.

So, the next time you find yourself asking "Why me?" consider asking a different question: "How might God use this?" It's not an easy shift to make, but it's one that can transform your perspective and bring meaning to even the darkest moments.

Through Christ, we are never alone in our suffering. He walks with us, sustains us, and gives our pain a purpose that reaches far beyond what we could ever imagine.

THE GLORY THAT AWAITS

While we may never fully understand the reasons for our suffering in this life, we can rest in the promise that it is not in vain. Romans 8:18 reminds us: "For I consider that the sufferings of this present time are not worth comparing with the glory that is to be revealed to us."

The trials we endure now are preparing us for something far greater —a glory that will eclipse every tear, every heartache, and every loss. When Christ returns, He will wipe away every tear, heal every wound, and make all things new. Remember the *Chronicles of Narnia* quote:

> *Wrong will be right, when Aslan comes in sight,*
> *At the sound of his roar, sorrows will be no more,*
> *When he bares his teeth, winter meets its death,*
> *And when he shakes his mane, we shall have spring again.*

Just as Aslan's return restores Narnia, Christ's return will bring renewal to our broken world. This is the hope we cling to—the promise that sustains us through the darkest valleys.

A Call to Endure

We may not choose suffering, but if it comes, we have a choice in how we respond. Will we allow it to draw us closer to Christ, the suffering Savior who endured the cross for us? Or will we let it embitter us and pull us away from Him?

Jesus thought it was worth it to suffer for us. Do we think it's worth it to suffer for Him and for the sake of others? By His grace, may we endure with faith, trusting that every trial is shaping us into His image and pointing others to His love. One day, when we stand before Him, all the pain will fade in the light of His glory. Until then, we press on, holding fast to the promise that He will make all things new.

Chapter 8

He Gives Us the Comforter

I want to talk about bullying. Not just the kind that happens in school hallways or on playgrounds, but the kind that happens in life. Because whether we recognize it or not, we all face a bully—one who never grows tired, never gives up, and never plays fair.

When I was a kid, I was bullied. Miriam was bullied too. Maybe you've been there. Maybe someone made you feel small, like you didn't belong, like you weren't worth standing up for. The damage from that kind of treatment lingers. It shapes how we see the world and ourselves. It can make us cautious, withdrawn, even paralyzed in fear of stepping into who we're meant to be. I sometimes wonder—if I hadn't been bullied, would I have been more outgoing, more confident, less hesitant to take risks?

Miriam's experience was even worse. It got to the point where we had to intervene, to remove her from that situation before it broke her completely. But what troubled me even more was how the school handled it. I remember a specific incident—she was harassed on school property after hours. A staff member saw it happen. When we confronted her, she had the audacity to say, "It was after contract hours."

Let that sink in.

A child was being hurt, and because her shift had technically ended, she didn't feel responsible. That was the moment I realized the deep brokenness of the system. A system that prioritizes contracts over care. A system that turns a blind eye when it's inconvenient.

I contrast that with my experience in Texas schools, where teachers watched over kids long after the final bell rang. They knew that many children walked home alone. They knew that care wasn't something you clock in and out of. They knew that showing up mattered.

And that brings me to God, the Comforter.

God Doesn't Work on a Contract

We do not have a God who punches a timecard. He does not log in for a shift, perform His duties, and then disappear when the clock runs out. He is not bound by limited hours or conditions. He does not grow weary or distracted, nor does He delegate His care to someone else when things get inconvenient.

We live in a world where so many relationships are transactional. Employers keep you around only as long as you provide value. Friendships can feel conditional, dependent on convenience. Even in families, people can disappoint us, turn their backs on us, or withdraw their support when things get difficult. But God is not like that. He promises, "I will never leave you nor forsake you" (Hebrews 13:5), as well as, "The steadfast love of the Lord never ceases; His mercies never come to an end; they are new every morning; great is your faithfulness" (Lamentations 3:22-23).

God's faithfulness isn't a service we have to qualify for. His presence isn't subject to an expiration date. His love isn't rationed out in increments. He is our ever-present Comforter, our refuge and strength, "a very present help in trouble" (Psalm 46:1). When the world tells us we are on our own, that no one cares, that no one is coming—God is already there.

Yet, just like Miriam had a real, physical bully, we have one too.

The Real Enemy: A Relentless Bully

Scripture does not shy away from the reality of evil. It does not paint the world as a safe, neutral place. It tells us plainly: We have an enemy, and he is relentless.

Jesus called him a thief who comes "only to steal and kill and destroy" (John 10:10). From the moment humanity drew its first breath, he has been lurking, whispering deception, planting doubt, stirring fear. He has broken families, crushed dreams, poisoned minds, and turned hearts away from God. And he is not alone.

When Adam and Eve fell, they didn't just introduce sin into the world—they handed over their authority. They gave Satan dominion. They allowed him to set up his counterfeit kingdom. And with him came a second great enemy: death.

The Bible calls death the "last enemy to be destroyed" (1 Corinthians 15:26). Satan bullies us with temptation, shame, and lies that entangle and ensnare. Death bullies us with suffering, with grief, with the cruel reminder that time is fleeting and life is fragile. Every single day, these enemies whisper in our ears:

"You're not good enough."

"No one cares about you."

"You'll never change."

"You'll always be a failure."

"Why even try? It's hopeless."

We hear these lies, and if we're not careful, we start to believe them. They weigh us down like chains, suffocating the life out of us. And sometimes, we wonder—is this just how it is? Are we powerless against them? Are we left to fight alone?

Our Comforter and Defender

A friend of mine lived in a tough neighborhood growing up. There was a group of kids—seven and eight years old—who were constantly tormented by a gang of older boys. These bullies were bigger, stronger, and crueler. They ruled the playground, and the younger kids were helpless against them. Except for one thing.

There was a protector in the neighborhood.

Sixteen-year-old Tommy wasn't afraid of the bullies. Whenever he was around, they wouldn't dare touch the younger kids. They knew better. They knew Tommy would stand in the gap.

And when Tommy moved away? Their protection was gone. The bullies took over again. The younger kids whispered his name like a legend, wishing he would come back.

"If only Tommy were here..."

That's exactly how the Holy Spirit is for us—except He has not moved away. He is still here. He is still protecting, still defending, still standing in the gap.

We are walking through enemy territory, but we are not alone.

Jesus said, "I will not leave you as orphans; I will come to you" (John 14:18). He also said, "And I will ask the Father, and he will give you another Helper, to be with you forever" (John 14:16).

The Holy Spirit is our Defender. The Holy Spirit is our Comforter. The Holy Spirit is our Advocate. He stands between us and the enemy. He shields us from deception. He reminds us of the truth when Satan whispers lies.

The question is: Are we listening? Or are we still believing the voice of the bully? Because maybe, just maybe, we've been accepting defeat when victory is already ours. Maybe, just maybe, we've been letting the enemy define us instead of listening to the One who created us.

Maybe it's time to stop living like orphans when we've been given a Father. Maybe it's time to stop hiding from the fight when we've been given a Protector. Maybe it's time to stop believing the lies when we've been given the Truth.

A Challenge for You

Take a moment. Sit in stillness. Ask yourself:

Where have I believed the enemy's lies?

Where have I felt abandoned, even though God has been there the whole time?

Where have I let fear paralyze me when the Holy Spirit was offering strength?

Write down your answers. Name the places where the bully has held power over you. Then, speak the truth of God over them.

Write Psalm 46:1 next to your fears: "God is our refuge and strength, a very present help in trouble."

Write John 14:18 next to your doubts: "I will not leave you as orphans; I will come to you."

Write Romans 8:37 next to your failures: "In all these things we are more than conquerors through Him who loved us."

The Comforter is here. The Advocate is here. The Defender is here. The enemy is loud, but God is louder. The bullies are strong, but God is stronger.

And you? You are never alone.

WHY DOESN'T GOD INTERVENE MORE?

There is an age-old question that we might as well tackle: If God loves us, why does He allow suffering? The first answer I have to offer is one we often overlook: We have no idea how many disasters He has already prevented. What would this world be like if God never intervened? If He removed His presence completely? If His people weren't praying, weren't loving, weren't pushing back against the darkness?

It would be hell.

God's presence is already restraining evil. His Spirit, working through His people, is already bringing light where there is darkness.

The second answer has to do with free will. God does not force love. He does not force obedience. He leads us, but He does not coerce us. He invites us to choose Him, to trust Him, to walk with Him.

But He never abandons us.

WALKING BY THE SPIRIT

The Bible gives us two options for how we can walk through our lives: walking by the flesh or walking by the Spirit (Romans 8:5-6).

When we walk by the flesh—when we let fear control us, when we believe the enemy's lies, when we act as though we are alone—we step outside of our Comforter's protection.

But when we walk by the Spirit—when we lean into His presence, listen for His voice, and trust His guidance—we experience peace, strength, and resilience, even in suffering.

"Resist the devil, and he will flee from you" (James 4:7). The Holy Spirit doesn't just comfort us in our suffering—He empowers us to overcome it.

A Story of Redemption: Cindy's Journey

Cindy didn't believe in therapy. She thought it was a waste of time.

But when she finally entered rehab, the staff suggested art therapy. Cindy resisted at first, thinking, *What good could painting do? It won't fix me.* But she gave in.

One day, she molded a figure out of clay—an operating table with herself lying underneath it. That's when it hit her. She felt trapped by her medically induced addiction, just like the figurine was trapped under the operating table. She had been trying to run from her pain, from the source of her brokenness, from the root of her addiction, but she remained stuck.

It was a breakthrough moment.

She began attending group sessions. She started seeing her struggles clearly. And she realized—God had never abandoned her. He had been walking beside her the whole time. She just hadn't been looking for Him.

How often is that true for us?

God is there. He has always been there. He is the non-anxious presence, the faithful Father, the Comforter who never clocks out.

The question is—are we walking with Him?

A Challenge for You

Where have you been trying to go it alone? Where have you believed the lie that God has abandoned you?

I challenge you: Write it down.

Take a piece of paper or a journal and write down the areas where you feel most alone. Then, pray over each one. Ask the Holy Spirit to meet you there. Ask Him to remind you of His presence.

You are not an orphan. You are not abandoned. You have a Comforter.

And He is here to stay.

CHAPTER 9

HE GIVES US HELP FROM HIS WORD

MORE THAN WE CAN HANDLE

There's a phrase that gets thrown around a lot in Christian circles, something people say when they don't know what else to say. It usually comes out when someone is suffering, overwhelmed, or facing an impossible situation. Maybe you've heard it. Maybe someone said it to you when your world was crumbling.

"God never gives you more than you can handle."

It sounds comforting, but it's not true. Nowhere in Scripture does God promise that life will never be too much for us. Nowhere does He say that we'll always have the strength to face our trials on our own. In fact, He says the opposite.

The verse people often misquote is 1 Corinthians 10:13 (NIV):

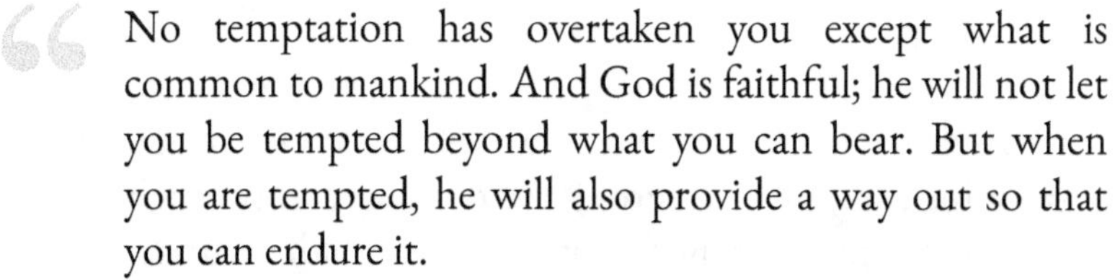

No temptation has overtaken you except what is common to mankind. And God is faithful; he will not let you be tempted beyond what you can bear. But when you are tempted, he will also provide a way out so that you can endure it.

God won't let us be tempted more than what we can bear. Instead, he provides the way to endure it. Paul was talking about resisting sin, not suffering. God will always provide a way to stand against temptation, but when it comes to trials, grief, and suffering? He absolutely gives us more than we can handle.

Look at the great men and women of the Bible. Job lost everything—his children, his wealth, his health—until he was sitting in the ashes, scraping his sores with broken pottery. Moses, standing before a burning bush, begged God to send someone else, because he felt completely inadequate. David, the mighty king, spent years running for his life, crying out to God in desperation. Paul despaired of life itself. Even Jesus, in the Garden of Gethsemane, fell to His knees under the weight of what was coming.

God allows suffering that is beyond our ability to endure alone so that we are driven to Him. If we were strong enough to handle everything life threw at us, why would we need a Savior? If we could carry our burdens on our own, why would we need a Comforter?

THE WORD OF GOD: OUR STRENGTH IN THE STORM

God's help doesn't always come in the way we expect. Sometimes, we want an immediate rescue, a miraculous intervention, a dramatic shift in circumstances. But more often than not, God's help comes in something He's already given us—His Word.

> All Scripture is breathed out by God and profitable for teaching, for reproof, for correction, and for training in righteousness.
>
> — 2 TIMOTHY 3:16

> For whatever was written in former days was written for our instruction, that through endurance and through the encouragement of the Scriptures we might have hope.
>
> — ROMANS 15:4

Hope. Strength. Encouragement. Endurance. This is what Scripture offers us.

Cindy and I have been through dark seasons—times when it felt like the walls were closing in, when suffering seemed relentless, when we were too exhausted to even pray. In those moments, the Bible was our lifeline. Not just a book to read, but a weapon to fight with, a comfort in the storm, a voice of truth when everything else felt uncertain.

God has not left us alone to navigate life's hardships without direction. He has given us His own words, written for us, preserved through time, passed down through generations so that when the storm comes— and it will come—we have something firm to hold onto.

Crying Out to God in the Psalms

Pain is not new. Sometimes we think our suffering isolates us, that no one else could possibly understand what we're going through. But the Bible tells a different story. The Psalms are filled with the raw, unfiltered cries of people who were suffering, struggling, and desperate for God's help.

David, the man after God's own heart, wrote Psalm 22—words that would later be echoed by Jesus on the cross: "My God, my God, why have you forsaken me? Why are you so far from saving me, from the words of my groaning?" (Psalm 22:1 NIV).

Ever felt like that?

David doesn't hold back. He tells God exactly how he feels—forgotten, abandoned, surrounded by enemies. But as the Psalm continues, his lament turns to trust:

> For he has not despised or abhorred
>   the affliction of the afflicted,
> and he has not hidden his face from him,
>   but has heard, when he cried to him.

— Psalm 22:24

This is a pattern we see throughout the Psalms—honest pain, followed by remembrance of who God is, followed by hope.

Psalm 42 is another example:

> Why are you cast down, O my soul, and why are you in turmoil within me? Hope in God; for I shall again praise him, my salvation and my God.

> — Psalm 42:5-6

This is what the Word of God does. In it, God gives us permission to be honest about our struggles, but also reminds us of the truth when we're tempted to believe the lies of the enemy.

A Story of Healing: Praying the Psalms

There was a pastor in Boston—a strong, faithful man, someone who had spent years ministering to others, walking with them through their darkest moments, pointing them toward God. But now, he was the one in crisis.

Depression had settled over him like a thick, suffocating fog. At first, he brushed it off as exhaustion, the natural weariness of ministry. But it wasn't just tiredness. It was something deeper, something heavier. He felt numb. Prayer felt hollow. Worship felt distant. Even opening his Bible felt like an obligation rather than a source of life.

He tried everything he knew to fight the feelings. Counseling. Rest. Medical evaluations. Long walks. Books. Encouragement from friends. He even considered stepping away from ministry altogether, thinking maybe he was no longer fit to lead. But nothing seemed to change the deep emptiness inside him.

One day, an older, wiser pastor—one who had been through his own share of valleys—sat him down and said something simple:

"Pray the Psalms."

The younger pastor nodded. "I do," he said.

"No." The older man shook his head. "I mean really pray them. Not just one or two, not just here and there. I want you to pray twenty-five Psalms a day. Out loud. Every day. For a month."

"That's...a lot," the pastor said.

"Do you want to get better?"

"Yes, of course."

"Then do it."

The pastor left that meeting skeptical. Twenty-five Psalms a day? It seemed excessive, overwhelming even. He wasn't sure he had the energy or focus for it. But he had nothing left to lose. So the next morning, he sat in his quiet living room, opened his Bible, and began.

At first, it was just words.

The first few Psalms felt mechanical, like reading through a script. He was reciting ancient prayers, but they didn't feel like his prayers. He wasn't sure it was doing anything.

But by the third or fourth Psalm, something shifted.

The words started to sink in. He found himself slowing down, lingering over phrases that spoke to his exhaustion.

"How long, O Lord? Will you forget me forever?" (Psalm 13:1).

That hit home. That was exactly how he felt.

He read it again, this time as a personal plea.

"How long, O Lord?" *How long will I feel this way?* "Will You forget me forever?"

He continued to other Psalms.

"The Lord is near to the brokenhearted and saves the crushed in spirit" (Psalm 34:18).

Tears welled up in his eyes. "Lord, I need You to be near. I am crushed in spirit. Be near to me."

By the time he reached Psalm 50, something strange happened—he wasn't just reading anymore. He was praying. He was crying out. He was worshiping.

And as the days passed, something even stranger happened.

The fog began to lift.

Not all at once. It wasn't some overnight miracle. But every day, he felt a little lighter. Every morning, the Psalms spoke more deeply to him. He was no longer just reciting Scripture—he was being transformed by it.

By the end of the month, he wasn't just praying the Psalms out of discipline. He was praying them out of need.

He wasn't just reading about God's faithfulness—he was experiencing it.

His depression didn't disappear entirely. Life was still hard. Ministry was still exhausting. But the deep, paralyzing emptiness had faded. Hope had returned.

He later told others, "I thought I needed a solution. But what I really needed was Scripture. I needed to soak in God's Word until it changed me."

That's the power of God's Word. It doesn't always change our circumstances, but it changes us. It rewires our thoughts, redirects our focus, and lifts our eyes from despair to hope.

It reminds us that we are not alone.

If you are in a dark place, if your soul feels dry, if you feel far from God—try this. Open your Bible. Read the Psalms. Pray them out loud. Let them become your prayers. Give God room to work in you through His Word.

Because He will.

PRAYING SCRIPTURE: A PRACTICAL GUIDE

The Psalms aren't the only parts of Scripture you can pray. The entire Bible can be turned into prayer. Every word, every promise, every story in Scripture is meant to shape not just what we believe but how we talk to God.

I remember a time when fear gripped me so tightly that I couldn't find the words to pray. My mind was racing, my heart felt heavy, and when I tried to pray, all I could manage was, "God, help me." It felt weak, empty, like I wasn't saying enough. But then I opened my Bible. I turned to Luke 8:22-25, the story of Jesus calming the storm. And suddenly, I realized—I didn't have to come up with the perfect words. The words were already there.

Instead of just reading the passage, I prayed through it.

"Jesus, You got into the boat with Your disciples. Lord, get into my boat. Be in my life, in my struggles, in my storm. The storm came, and the disciples were afraid. Lord, I feel like that. My life is storming around me, and I'm afraid. I don't know what's coming next, and it feels overwhelming. The disciples cried out, and You calmed the storm. Jesus, I cry out to You now—speak peace over my storm. Rebuke the winds and waves in my life. Remind me that You are greater than my fears. You asked them, 'Where is your faith?' Lord, help me trust You more. Strengthen my faith when I am weak. Help me to remember that You are with me."

I can't explain it, but something changed as I prayed those words. My fear didn't vanish instantly, but I felt steadier. I felt like I wasn't alone in the storm. And I realized something—praying Scripture isn't just about asking God for things. It's about reminding ourselves of who He is.

When we pray Scripture, we are stepping into something bigger than our own limited perspective. We are praying the very words God has already spoken, aligning our hearts with His truth instead of our fears.

Why This Matters

I've met many people who hesitate to pray because they don't know what to say. They think their prayers need to be long, eloquent, or profound. But the truth is, God has already given us the words. When we pray Scripture, we don't have to come up with anything new—we just have to take what He has said and make it personal.

Maybe you're carrying guilt from a past mistake. You don't know how to ask for forgiveness, and you wonder if God could really still love you. Open to Psalm 51 and pray David's words as your own:

"Have mercy on me, O God, according to Your steadfast love" (v. 1).

"Wash me thoroughly from my iniquity, and cleanse me from my sin" (v. 2).

"Create in me a clean heart, O God, and renew a right spirit within me" (v. 10).

Or maybe you're facing a season of loss. You don't have the strength to form your own words. Let Psalm 23 be your prayer:

"Lord, You are my shepherd—I don't know what's next, but I trust You will guide me."

"Even though I walk through the valley of the shadow of death, I will fear no evil, for You are with me" (v. 4).

See how this works? We aren't just reading the Bible—we're praying it. We're taking God's promises and speaking them over our lives, believing that what He said then is still true today.

A Challenge for You

If you're going through a hard season—or if you simply want to grow in your relationship with God—try this for the next seven days.

Open your Bible. Find a passage that speaks to where you are right now. Maybe it's a Psalm. Maybe it's something Jesus said. Maybe it's a promise from Isaiah. Whatever it is, don't just read it—pray it.

Let it shape your words. Let it steady your heart. Let it remind you that God is near, and His Word is alive.

You don't have to struggle through prayer, wondering if you're saying the right things. God has already given you the words. Now, all you have to do is pray them.

He Gives Us Hope and Healing

The Agony of Detox and the Hope of a New Beginning

The summer of Cindy's detox was one of the longest and most painful seasons of our lives. Her body, so dependent on pain medications, was now in full rebellion. Not only did she have to endure the pain the drugs had once masked, but her body, desperate for its chemical fix, created new pain in places that had never hurt before. It was as if every nerve was firing off alarms, every muscle and joint screaming for relief. Her mind was clouded, her emotions raw, and her temper short. She was angry—so angry that I sometimes wondered if I would ever see the woman I married again.

Every day, she wanted to give up. Every day, she told me she couldn't do it. And every day, I told her to hold on for just one more. I absorbed the brunt of her frustration, her fury, her despair. But I also knew that if she gave in, if she relapsed, all the pain of detox would have been for nothing. And so I kept pushing her forward, one painful step at a time.

Then, one day, something changed.

HOPE BREAKS THROUGH

It was the Tuesday after Labor Day when my phone rang. I hesitated before answering, bracing myself for another conversation laced with anger and hopelessness. But then I heard it—her voice. It was calm. It was clear. It was the Cindy I remembered, the Cindy I had been waiting to hear for almost a decade.

"I'm ready to come home," she said.

At first, I didn't know what to say. After so many years of chaos, could this really be happening? Could she finally be free?

I left work early and drove to the hospital to pick her up, half expecting to find the same broken woman I had dropped off weeks before. But when she walked through those doors, I knew something had changed. Her eyes were clear. Her movements were steady. And for the first time in far too long, our future looked brighter.

THE LONG ROAD TO RECOVERY

Opiate addiction is no small thing. It is a beast that takes hold of a person and refuses to let go. Even though Cindy had made it through detox, even though she had endured the worst of the physical withdrawal, her journey was far from over. The body might heal, but the mind takes longer. The wounds addiction leaves on a person—and on the people who love them—don't fade overnight.

Around the same time Cindy came home, our church was launching a Celebrate Recovery chapter. I had been asked to help with the technical aspects of the ministry, and as I sat in those early meetings, listening to testimonies of healing and redemption, I knew Cindy needed to be part of it. She wasn't just recovering from addiction; she was recovering from years of pain, loss, and brokenness. She needed a place where she could process, where she could heal, where she could find community again.

And so, hesitant but willing, she walked through the doors of Celebrate Recovery.

That was when Jesus began her true deliverance.

The Cost of Addiction

As much as I wanted to believe that Cindy's return home would be the beginning of everything going back to normal, the truth was far more complicated. Addiction doesn't just hurt the person caught in its grip—it tears apart families.

For Phoebe, Cindy's addiction had stolen her childhood. All she could remember was a mother who was distant, volatile, and unpredictable. The love was buried beneath years of emotional wounds, and Phoebe had built walls around her heart to keep from being hurt again.

Even though Cindy was changing, even though she was trying to rebuild what had been lost, Phoebe couldn't simply erase the past. In her phone, Cindy's contact name had been changed from "Mom" to "Cindy." And whenever she spoke about her, it was with detachment—"she" or "her," never "Mom."

Cindy didn't understand. Now that she was sober, she wanted to move forward, to put everything behind them. But wounds that deep don't heal overnight. I had to remind Cindy, over and over, that forgiveness is a process. That trust, once broken, takes time to rebuild. That just because she had been freed from addiction didn't mean the past had disappeared.

It would take years, but I can say now, looking back, that God did restore their relationship. Slowly, Phoebe allowed Cindy back into her life. Slowly, the walls came down. And one day, Cindy heard something she had been longing to hear for years:

"Mom."

God's Healing: More Than Physical

The Bible makes it clear: Healing is part of God's plan for us. Physical healing, yes, but also emotional and spiritual healing. We are all in need of restoration.

For Cindy, her battle wasn't just with addiction. It was with the trauma buried deep inside her. In 1996, long before addiction took hold, a memory resurfaced that nearly shattered her. The human brain has a way of protecting itself—hiding the most painful experiences until, one day, they rise to the surface. That was the year Cindy's mind finally allowed her to remember her rape.

It wasn't something she had ever spoken about. It had been buried so deep that even she had forgotten. But then, one night, I snapped my belt —just playing around with the dogs, like I had done so many times before.

Cindy froze. Terror filled her eyes. And suddenly, she wasn't in our living room anymore—she was back there, back in that moment, back in the nightmare. She became afraid of me. She became afraid of every man. Her mind projected the face of her attacker onto mine. She couldn't even sleep in the same room as me. It was one of the hardest things I've ever had to walk through.

God is a healer—not just of bodies, but of hearts and minds. Through nearly a year of counseling, through the hard work of facing the past, Cindy found freedom. One of the most powerful moments of that journey was the day she wrote a letter to her attacker. She poured out everything—her anger, her pain, her grief. She held nothing back. And then, when she was ready, we burned it.

Watching those pages turn to ash was a moment of victory. Cindy was no longer a prisoner to that past.

GOD'S PROMISE OF HOPE

Looking back at everything Cindy endured—the addiction, the trauma, the pain, the surgeries, the loss—it would be easy to focus only on the suffering. To let it define her story. To believe that pain was all there was. But that's not where the story ends.

Because through it all, God was there.

Through every moment of darkness, He was there.

Through every season of pain, He was working.

Through every hopeless night, He was whispering, "Hold on. I'm not finished yet."

The enemy wants us to believe that suffering is the final word. That the weight of our struggles is too great. That the wounds we carry will never heal. That the things we have lost can never be restored. He wants us to believe that our past disqualifies us from the future God has for us.

But the truth is this: There is hope.

There is healing.

There is life on the other side of the storm.

For Cindy, healing didn't happen overnight. It took time. It took effort. It took surrender. There were moments of doubt, days of discouragement, and nights when it seemed like the pain would never end. But she kept going and kept believing. She kept trusting that God was not done with her story.

And she healed.

Not because she was strong enough, but because God was.

Not because she had all the answers, but because He did.

Not because she had everything figured out, but because she had a Savior who never let her go.

And if He did it for her, He can do it for you.

Never Give Up

Maybe right now, you are walking through your own season of pain. Maybe you are carrying wounds that feel too deep to heal. Maybe you've been fighting the same battle for so long that you wonder if freedom is even possible.

Hold on.

If you feel trapped in addiction, there is freedom.

If your body is sick, there is healing.

If your heart is broken, there is restoration.

If your mind is weary, there is peace.

God has not abandoned you. Even when He feels distant, even when the prayers seem to go unanswered, even when the suffering makes no sense—He is with you.

You are not alone. Healing is possible. Restoration is possible. Redemption is possible. Sometimes, the road to healing is long. Sometimes, it's one agonizing step at a time. Sometimes, you will feel like you're walking in the dark, unsure of what's ahead. But don't stop. Keep going. Keep fighting. Keep believing, because your story isn't over yet; God is still writing it.

And what He restores, He restores completely. What He heals, He makes whole. What He redeems, He redeems fully.

So don't give up.

Not today. Not ever.

The Gift of Community

In the next chapter, I want to talk about one of the greatest gifts God gives us on the journey to healing: community.

Suffering often makes us feel isolated, as if no one else could possibly understand. But God never intended for us to walk through trials alone. He gives us His people—brothers and sisters in Christ—to encourage us, pray for us, and help carry the burdens that feel too heavy to bear.

Healing happens in relationships. Freedom is found in connection. Strength is renewed when we lean on the body of Christ.

So as we move forward, let's talk about what it means to walk this journey together.

CHAPTER 11

HE GIVES US COMMUNITY AND SUPPORT

THE BEGINNING OF A PERSONALITY SHIFT

One day, Cindy lashed out at Jacob and Phoebe, and something in me froze. It wasn't just that she yelled—it was how she did it, the way her voice cut through the air like a blade. The way the children shrank back, their laughter dying instantly, replaced by fear. I had never seen Cindy like that before.

I don't remember exactly what set her off. The kids had been playing, cutting up like children do, their energy filling the hospital room where we were visiting. One moment, they were giggling. The next minute, Cindy's voice was booming, sharp with irritation and rage.

Both kids immediately started crying. But Cindy didn't stop. She kept shouting, her anger flaring into something unrecognizable. That was when I knew—it was time to go.

I didn't understand it at the time. I just knew something was wrong. When Jacob and Phoebe asked me why their mother had yelled at them like that, I had no answers. I knelt down, wrapped them both in my arms, and whispered, "I don't know."

It wasn't until years later that I learned how opiates affect the brain, how prolonged use can strip away a person's ability to regulate emotions, leaving them raw, erratic, and unpredictable. I didn't realize at the time that Cindy's outburst wasn't entirely her—it was the drugs speaking, the pain speaking, the exhaustion speaking. But to a child, none of that mattered. All they knew was that their mother had changed.

When Cindy was stable enough, she was transferred to a long-term acute care (LTAC) facility. She still needed constant medical attention but no longer required the immediate presence of doctors. It was a small step toward progress, but it was still a grueling season for our family.

The LTAC was forty-five minutes away from home, and I drove back and forth every chance I got. Every visit, I held onto the hope that Cindy would be a little better, a little more like herself. Some days, she was. Other days, she wasn't. But no matter what, we kept going. We kept showing up.

THE STRENGTH OF COMMUNITY

During this time, something remarkable happened.

Our church family surrounded us in ways we never expected. They didn't just offer words of encouragement; they showed up—again and again. Meals appeared at our doorstep, prepared by hands that understood we were too exhausted to cook. Friends stepped in to help with the kids. Even simple texts of encouragement lifted burdens I didn't realize I was carrying.

One Sunday morning, as we were getting ready for church, Mary and I talked about picking up another couple of meals to stock the freezer. From the back seat, Phoebe, who was only five years old at the time, piped up with a question that struck me to my core.

"How do people without a church family make it through hard times?"

I sat in silence for a moment, her words hanging in the air.

How do they?

How do people walk through suffering without a body of believers to hold them up when they can't stand on their own? How do they endure pain without a community to lift their burdens? How do they find hope when they are completely alone?

I didn't have an answer. But I did know this: We would not have survived without the church.

Small Blessings in a Dark Time

Looking back, I see how many blessings we were given in that season—small ones, big ones, unnoticed ones. My boss at the school district was one of them. She knew my home situation, and instead of making my life harder, she gave me the flexibility I needed. She let me make up time on weekends, gave me grace when I had to leave early, and never once made me feel like my job was at risk.

At the time, I was just trying to get through each day. But now, I see that God was weaving together provision in ways I couldn't recognize then.

But there was also darkness.

Cindy's verbal and emotional abuse toward me and the kids had become relentless. I didn't understand why. I thought addiction looked like illicit drugs in dark alleys, not pharmaceuticals prescribed by doctors. I had no idea that pain medications could alter a person's personality, their emotions, their very soul. And because I didn't understand it, I couldn't know how to begin to fix it.

I wish I had known then what I know now. Ignorance is costly, and our family paid the price.

Still, through it all, our church stood beside us.

The Church at Its Best (and Worst)

If you are walking through suffering and you do not have a church family, find one. I say that with urgency, because even if you're not in a difficult season now, it's guaranteed that hard times will come. They come for all of us. When they do, you will need people who step in when you can't keep going on your own.

The Bible describes the early church, which is a beautiful picture of what the church should continue to be.

All the believers were together and had everything in common. They sold property and possessions to give to anyone who had need.

— ACTS 2:44-45 NIV

That's what we experienced. People giving. People serving without expecting anything in return. People living out God's design for the church.

But as much as the church can be a place of healing, it can also be a place of wounds.

Not everyone was supportive. Rumors began to spread—about Cindy, about me, about our kids. People whispered. They stared. They speculated about what had really happened in our home, about what kind of parents we were.

Cindy felt the weight of it deeply. It became too much, and she eventually stopped coming to church altogether. But I couldn't stop coming—I was responsible for all the audio services in the building. Every Sunday, I showed up, standing in the back, feeling the weight of eyes on me.

And then, one day, it all stopped.

It was as if, suddenly, our suffering was acceptable because our story had reached a "happy ending."

That was a hard lesson to learn.

If you are part of a church, be very careful with your words. Gossip is easy. It feels harmless. But it can destroy people. It can make suffering even harder than it already is.

Paul warned about this in Romans:

You, then, why do you judge your brother or sister? Or why do you treat them with contempt? For we will all stand before God's judgment seat.

— ROMANS 14:10 NIV

There's a lot that I don't remember from those years. But I will never forget who stood beside us—and who didn't.

Celebrate Recovery: A Lifeline

If there was one thing that saved Cindy's life, besides Jesus Himself, it was Celebrate Recovery.

As I mentioned, by the time she got involved, I had already been helping with the technical side of things at church. I had listened to the testimonies. I had seen what true, raw, unfiltered healing looked like. And I knew Cindy needed it.

Celebrate Recovery doesn't just help people break addictions—it gives them a family. A sponsor. A community of people who understand. You never walk through it alone.

When Cindy walked through those doors, she was no longer just fighting addiction—she was stepping into healing.

CHAPTER 12

HE GIVES US PROVISION

THE ROLLER COASTER OF NEED AND PROVISION

Life brought relentless ups and downs. Hospital stays, medical bills, job struggles—each day seemed to bring another crisis. Our finances spiraled out of control. Every hospitalization meant more medical debt; every doctor's visit, another bill we couldn't pay. There were moments when I stared at the stack of statements on the table, knowing there was no way to stretch what little we had to cover what we owed. And it wasn't just the big things; even daily necessities felt overwhelming. Fast food became a staple because I didn't have the time or energy to cook after work. Our grocery budget was whatever was left over after everything else. Some days, that meant nothing.

To try and make ends meet, I had taken on contract work for another school district. It wasn't much, but it helped. At least, I thought it would—until my employer at the time (not the compassionate boss from the previous chapter) discovered my side work. One day between Christmas and New Year's, while we were in Colorado, my boss called. He started questioning my contract work, suggesting there was a conflict of interest, as if I was trying to sell a competing system. I wasn't. But no one would listen. I was ordered to stop immediately. No discussion. No consideration for the fact that I was just trying to provide for my family.

With that extra income gone, I felt the pressure mounting. How were we supposed to make it? I prayed for provision, but I also worked as hard as I could. The days blurred into exhaustion. Work, hospital visits, bills, uncertainty—on repeat.

Somehow, we always had enough to survive.

The Hidden Hand of God

At the time, it felt like we were barely treading water. I couldn't see the pattern, the way God was orchestrating provision behind the scenes. But looking back, I can see it so clearly now—He was there in every moment, even when I didn't recognize it.

He was in the meals that church members delivered to our door when I had no idea what we were going to eat that night. He was in the simple fact that, despite the overwhelming odds, we never lost everything.

It reminds me of another time God provided just enough, not too much, not too little, but enough to get through the day.

Manna in the Wilderness: Daily Trust in a Faithful God

The Israelites knew what it was like to wake up every morning not knowing how they were going to survive. After escaping Egypt, they found themselves in the wilderness, with nothing but uncertainty stretching before them. No food. No farms. No way to provide for themselves.

Then God did something extraordinary. We read about it in Exodus 16. He sent manna—bread from heaven. Every morning, they would wake up and find the ground covered in it. But there was a rule: They could only gather enough for that day. If they tried to store extra, it would rot. They had to trust that when tomorrow came, the manna would be there again.

This was God's way of teaching them—and us—that provision is not about stockpiling resources; it's about trusting the Provider.

I didn't always see it back then, but I was living this lesson every day. God didn't give me a windfall that solved all our problems. Instead, He gave me enough for today. And then He did it again tomorrow. And the next day.

THE WIDOW'S JAR: WHEN GOD STRETCHES THE LITTLE WE HAVE

In 1 Kings 17, we read about a widow in Zarephath who was on the brink of starvation. There was a famine in the land, and she had almost nothing left—just a handful of flour and a little oil. Enough for one last meal before she and her son would prepare to die.

Then the prophet Elijah arrived. He asked her for something unthinkable—to make him bread first before feeding herself and her child. It was an absurd request. But she obeyed. And that's when the miracle happened. "The jar of flour was not spent, neither did the jug of oil become empty, according to the word of the Lord that he spoke by Elijah" (1 Kings 17:16).

Her jar never ran out.

There were times during those hard years when I felt like we were down to our last handful of flour. But somehow, God stretched it. Somehow, the bills didn't crush us completely. Somehow, Cindy's medical needs were covered when they should have buried us. Somehow, we made it.

This is how God works. He doesn't always provide in advance, but He provides as we go.

MULTIPLICATION IN THE HANDS OF JESUS

Of course, the greatest example of God's provision is seen in a miracle Jesus performed.

When thousands of hungry people gathered to hear Him teach, the disciples panicked. They had nothing to feed them. Just a few loaves of bread and some fish. It wasn't enough.

Or so it seemed.

According to Matthew 14, Mark 6, Luke 9, and John 6, Jesus took that small meal, blessed it, broke it, and multiplied it. The little they had became more than enough. That's exactly what God does in our lives. He takes the little we have, the last bit of strength, the last paycheck, the last ounce of faith, and He multiplies it. He makes it more than enough.

Your Call to Trust the God Who Provides

If you're in a season where provision seems scarce, where the weight of financial strain, job insecurity, or an uncertain future looms over you like a storm cloud, I want you to know—you are not alone.

I have walked this road. I have felt the deep pit in my stomach when checking the bank account and realizing there wasn't enough to cover the bills. I have stared at medical statements, hospital invoices, and overdue notices, wondering how in the world we were supposed to make it. I have wrestled with the kind of exhaustion that settles in your bones when you carry a burden that doesn't seem to lighten, when no amount of budgeting, no side job, no desperate attempt to stretch a paycheck seems to be enough.

But here's what I've learned through it all: God is already working on your behalf.

It may not feel or look like it. But His provision is coming because He is a God who sees.

When Hagar fled into the wilderness, carrying nothing but despair and her son, convinced that they would die, God saw her. He heard her cries. He called out to her, provided water, and opened her eyes to see what she had not seen before. And she called Him El-Roi—"The God who sees me" (Genesis 16:13 NIV).

The same God who saw Hagar sees you.

Maybe you're waiting for a financial windfall when God is sending daily manna. Maybe you're hoping for a massive breakthrough when God is keeping your jar of oil from running dry, providing just enough for today. Maybe you feel like what you have—your time, your energy, your resources—is far too small, when in the hands of Jesus, it is more than enough.

So what do you do when you are in a season of lack? When the weight of your circumstances feels crushing? Here's what I have learned.

1. Trust God for Today.

God doesn't ask you to figure out next month, next week, or even tomorrow. He asks you to trust Him for today.

The Israelites were not allowed to store up extra manna for tomorrow. Why? Because God was teaching them to trust that when the sun rose again, He would be there.

Jesus echoed this same truth when He said, "Do not worry about tomorrow, for tomorrow will worry about itself" (Matthew 6:34 NIV).

This doesn't mean we don't plan or make wise choices. But it does mean that we stop borrowing trouble from a future we don't control. God's mercy, His provision, His grace—they are fresh every morning (Lamentations 3:22-23).

He has been faithful today. He will be faithful tomorrow.

2. Give God What Little You Have.

Maybe you feel like what you have—your finances, your abilities, your strength—is too insignificant to make a difference. But in the hands of Jesus, small things become more than enough.

In a similar story to the one from earlier, the widow in 2 Kings 4 was on the verge of losing everything. She had nothing left but a little jar of oil. When she cried out to the prophet Elisha, he told her to pour it out —to gather every empty jar she could find and start filling them.

She obeyed. She took what little she had and poured it out, and God multiplied it. Every jar was filled until there were no empty jars left.

What if she had refused to pour? What if she had held onto the little she had, convinced it wasn't enough?

Sometimes, the miracle comes when we release the little we're holding onto. It may be a small act of generosity. It may be the last bit of faith you can muster. It may be stepping forward into an opportunity you don't feel qualified for. But in the hands of Jesus, small things multiply.

3. Remember How He Has Provided Before.

When we're in a difficult season, it's easy to forget. We forget the times God came through before. We forget the moments He provided when we had no idea how we were going to make it.

David, before facing Goliath, remembered. He looked back on the times God had delivered him from the lion and the bear, and that past faithfulness gave him confidence for the battle ahead (1 Samuel 17:34-37).

What has God already done for you? Where has He shown up before? Write it down. Speak it out loud. Remind yourself of His faithfulness. The more we reflect on His past provision, the easier it becomes to trust Him for what's ahead.

4. Stay Connected to Your Community.

One of the greatest mistakes we can make in difficult times is isolating ourselves. God often provides through people.

When we were at our lowest, our church family brought meals, encouraged us, and reminded us that we weren't alone. If we had withdrawn, if we had cut ourselves off from community, we would have missed out on the tangible ways God was providing.

You are not meant to do this alone. Lean on the people God has placed in your life.

5. Be Ready to Step Out in Faith.

The widow had to pour out the last of her oil before she saw the miracle. The Israelites had to step into the Red Sea before it parted. Peter had to step out of the boat before he walked on water.

Faith often requires action. Sometimes, obedience comes before the breakthrough.

If God is prompting you to move, to give, to take a step in faith—do it. Don't wait for the entire path to be clear before you take the first step. Provision is often waiting on the other side of obedience.

A FINAL ENCOURAGEMENT: THE GOD WHO NEVER FAILS

I don't know your exact situation right now. Maybe you're facing a mountain of debt, a job loss, a medical crisis, or an overwhelming uncertainty about your future. Maybe it feels like there is no way forward.

But here's what I can tell you: God is faithful.

I can say that with confidence because I have experienced His provision. I have been in a place where there were no answers, where everything seemed to be unraveling, where I didn't know how we were going to make it. And yet, God provided.

He may not do it in the way you expect. He may not do it in the timing you want. But He will care for you.

I look back on our story now, and I see—He was there the whole time. There was never a moment when we were truly abandoned. There was never a day when He left us without hope. There was never a situation where He wasn't making a way, even when we couldn't see it.

And if He did it for me, He will do it for you.

Maybe you're looking at the loaves and fish in your hands, convinced they're not enough. Maybe you're staring at the empty jar, wondering how it could possibly sustain you. Maybe you're standing in front of the sea, feeling trapped on all sides.

Hold on. Your story isn't over yet.

God is already at work. The answer is already on the way. The provision is already set in motion.

Keep going. Keep trusting. Keep believing.

He is Jehovah Jireh—the God who provides.

And He has never failed.

And He never will.

CHAPTER 13
____

FINAL THOUGHTS

As we look back over the journey we've shared in these pages—the pain, the loss, the struggles, the victories, the healing, and the unrelenting faithfulness of God—we're overwhelmed with gratitude. Not because the road was easy. It wasn't. Not because every prayer was answered the way we wanted. Many weren't. But because through it all, we have come to know, beyond any doubt, that God is real, present, and faithful.

Maybe you've seen yourself in some of our struggles. Maybe you've faced loss that felt impossible to endure. Maybe you've been caught in the cycle of addiction, or loved someone who was. Maybe you've felt abandoned, betrayed, or overwhelmed by circumstances beyond your control. If so, I want you to hear this clearly: You are not alone, and you are not without hope.

The same God who sustained us through every storm, who provided when we had nothing, who brought healing when we thought all was lost—that same God is with you, too.

THE CALL TO TRUST

We've talked a lot about suffering in this book, because suffering is an unavoidable part of life. Jesus Himself told us that "In this world you will have trouble. But take heart! I have overcome the world" (John 16:33 NIV). The Bible never promises that we won't face hardship, but it does promise that we never face it alone.

God is not distant. He's not a silent observer watching from the heavens, waiting to see if you can figure things out. He is near. He is present. He is active in your life even now, whether you feel it or not. The question is not whether God is with you—the question is whether you will choose to trust Him.

That trust is not always easy. When the bills pile up, when the diagnosis comes, when a relationship shatters, when everything you thought was secure is shaken—trusting God feels risky. It feels impossible at times. But this is what we've learned: God is trustworthy even when we don't understand Him.

We have seen His provision come at the last possible moment. We have seen healing when all hope seemed lost. We have seen Him redeem what was broken, restore what was stolen, and rebuild what we thought had crumbled beyond repair. If He can do it for us, He can do it for you.

CHOOSING TO WALK FORWARD

Maybe you've been stuck in survival mode for so long that you don't even know how to hope anymore. Maybe you feel like you've been through too much, that your faith is too weak, that your past is too heavy to move forward. But let me remind you—God does not call you to live in the past. He calls you forward.

Think about the Israelites. After centuries of slavery in Egypt, God miraculously delivered them. He split the Red Sea, led them by a pillar of fire, and provided manna from heaven. But what did they do? They longed for Egypt. They looked backward, complaining about the hardships of the wilderness, rather than trusting that God was leading them to the Promised Land.

How often do we do the same? How often do we let fear keep us from stepping into the freedom and healing God has for us?

God is calling you forward. That might mean surrendering something you've been clinging to—control, resentment, fear, addiction, self-sufficiency. It might mean making a step of faith, even when you don't know where it will lead. But He is always leading you toward life, toward wholeness, toward Him.

What Response Will You Choose?

This book has been about more than just our journey—it's about yours, too. You have a choice to make. Will you keep trying to manage life on your own, or will you surrender and trust the One who holds all things together?

If you're still wrestling, still struggling, still unsure, that's okay. God is not afraid of your questions, your doubts, or your fears. But don't let them keep you from taking the next step.

If you need healing, ask God for it. He may heal instantly, or He may take you on a journey, but He is still the Healer.

If you need provision, trust Him to provide. He sees every need and knows exactly what is required.

If you need restoration, surrender to His process. Healing takes time, but He is always working.

If you feel lost, lean into His Word. The Bible is full of stories of people just like you—broken, hurting, questioning—who found their answers in Him.

You don't have to figure everything out today. But you do need to take the next step.

The Invitation

At the end of it all, this is the most important truth: Jesus is enough.

No matter what life brings, no matter how deep the valley or how high the mountain, He is our source, our strength, our hope, and our salvation. And He is inviting you into deeper trust, deeper faith, and deeper relationship with Him.

So what will you do?

Will you let go of the weight you've been carrying and trust Him to carry it instead?

Will you take the next step, even if you don't see the whole path ahead?

Will you believe that, despite everything, God is still good, and He is still with you?

Because He is.

And He always will be.

www.ingramcontent.com/pod-product-compliance
Lightning Source LLC
Chambersburg PA
CBHW051544050726
47595CB00002B/635